# Management Accounting, Human Resource Policies and Organisational Performance in Canada, Japan and the UK

# Management Accounting, Human Resource Policies and Organisational Performance in Canada, Japan and the UK

Reza Kouhy
Glasgow Caledonian University, Scotland

Rishma Vedd
California State University, Northridge, USA

Takeo Yoshikawa
Graduate School of Hosei University, Japan

John Innes
University of Dundee, Scotland

AMSTERDAM • BOSTON • HEIDELBERG • LONDON
NEW YORK • OXFORD • PARIS • SAN DIEGO
SAN FRANCISCO • SINGAPORE • SYDNEY • TOKYO

CIMA Publishing is an imprint of Elsevier

CIMA Publishing is an imprint of Elsevier
The Boulevard, Langford Lane, Kidlington, Oxford, OX5 1GB, UK
30 Corporate Drive, Suite 400, Burlington, MA 01803, USA

First edition 2010

**British Library Cataloguing in Publication Data**
A catalogue record for this book is available from the British Library

**Library of Congress Cataloguing in Publication Data**
A catalog record for this book is available from the Library of Congress

ISBN–13: 978-0-08-096592-5

For information on all CIMA Publishing publications visit our
web site at books.elsevier.com

Typeset by Macmillan Publishing Solutions
www.macmillansolutions.com

Transferred to Digital Printing in 2009

Working together to grow
libraries in developing countries

www.elsevier.com | www.bookaid.org | www.sabre.org

ELSEVIER     BOOK AID
             International     Sabre Foundation

# Contents

# Acknowledgements

The authors wish to thank the Chartered Institute of Management Accountants for funding the research on which this report is based. We thank Kim Ansell, Jasmin Harvey and Kati Kuusisto of CIMA for all their administrative assistance with this project, Dick Brown of the University of Dundee for his statistical advice and two anonymous referees for their constructive comments. We are very grateful for all the time given by the accountants and managers during the six case studies and the 100 telephone interviews. Without their knowledge and assistance this research project would not have been possible. We dedicate this report to all our interviewees.

# About the Authors

**Reza Kouhy** is a professor of accounting at Glasgow Caledonian University. His main research interests are human resource accounting, oil and gas accounting and performance management.

**Rishma Vedd** is an assistant professor at California State University, Northridge. Her research interests include performance management and the interface between management accounting and strategic human resource management.

**Takeo Yoshikawa** is a professor of accounting at the Graduate School of Hosei University, emeritus professor of Yokohama National University and visiting professor at the University of Edinburgh. His research interests are cost and management accounting – in particular, cost management, activity-based costing and the balanced scorecard.

**John Innes** is an emeritus professor of the University of Dundee. His research interest is management accounting including activity-based costing, Japanese cost management and the role of management accountants in relation to management functions such as design and human resource management.

# Executive Summary

## 1. Objectives

This research project examined the relationships between human resource (HR) policies, management accounting and organisational performance on the basis of six case studies (two in Canada, two in Japan and two in the UK) and 100 telephone interviews (40 in Japan, 30 in Canada and 30 in the UK). This project was built on the results of a previous project funded by CIMA on management accounting and strategic HR management (Innes et al., 2001) by:

a. extending the research into the area of the relationship between different HR policies and organisational performance and, in particular, how management accountants help to establish links between HR policies and organisational performance;

b. extending the research into Japanese companies to give a different perspective and another point of comparison;

c. testing the case study results in a telephone survey.

## 2. Findings – Case Studies

The six case studies covered building materials, consumer products, electronics, software development, timber products and a utility. There were seven interviewees in each case with at least two management accountants, at least two HR managers and at least two managers with responsibility for some aspect of organisational performance. In all six cases, the average experience of the interviewees was at least 10 years. One company had existed for about 20 years but the other five had been operating for about 100 years. Employee costs as a percentage of total costs varied between 30% and 40% for five of the cases with one case (software development) being 70%.

### 2.1. Performance Measures

All six case studies used a mix of financial and non-financial performance measures – for example:

Case A – achievement of budget, growth, market share, sales per employee

Case B – cash flow, customer satisfaction, economic value added (EVA is a trademark of Stern, Stewart and Co.), employee morale, social contribution, sustainable growth

Case C – customer satisfaction, EVA, productivity, quadruple bottom line, quality, safety

Case D – delivery, environment, productivity, return on net assets, safety

Case E – cash flow, customer satisfaction, delivery, quality, sales

Case F – customer service, profitability, safety, total shareholder return

## 2.2.    Links between HR Managers and Management Accountants

In all six case studies, important links between HR managers and management accountants were the annual budget and long-term strategic plans. For example, key topics of discussion were the proposed number of employees, the required mix of skills and the budgeted salaries. In all six case studies, there were also regular meetings where management accountants discussed with HR managers comparisons of actual results against budgeted results with detailed analysis of the variances. Almost all the interviewees considered the verbal discussions with the management accountants to be at least as important as the written variance reports.

In Cases A, B, C and F, the HR managers and management accountants worked closely together on the performance-related bonus scheme. For example, in Cases B and C the management accountants interpreted the meaning of EVA reports for HR managers. In Cases A, B, C and F, the management accountants discussed the financial and non-financial performance measures used in the bonus scheme model with HR managers before the proposed bonus model was finalised and later interpreted the actual results from the bonus scheme.

Communication links also existed between HR managers and management accountants in relation to decision-making. For example, in Case C the management accountants calculated that Case C spent four times as much on workers' compensation as its competitors in the same industry. The HR managers and management accountants were now working together and had already managed to reduce very significantly Case C's workers' compensation payments. Similarly, in Case F, HR managers and management accountants had almost daily contact in a decision-making capacity.

## 2.3.    HR Policies and Organisational Performance

The HR policies mentioned by the interviewees as affecting organisational performance in at least three of the six case studies included:

a.   recruitment

b.   teamwork

c.   organisational culture (with regard to employees)

d. job for life

e. training

f. pensions.

Of course, interviewees in individual case studies mentioned other HR policies such as diversity and equality but the above six HR policies were highlighted in at least three of the six cases as having a direct effect on organisational performance. With the possible exception of the above job for life policy, different cultures did not appear to have a major impact on the efficacy of HR policies on organisational performance. In both the Japanese case studies, the culture of a job for life was important and encouraged managers to take a long-term view, increased organisational loyalty from employees, increased employee motivation and had a positive effect on organisational performance. However, one of the British cases also operated a form of job for life policy that also had a positive effect on organisational performance.

## 3. Findings – Telephone Interviews

After the six case studies were completed, a cross-case analysis was undertaken and 11 findings were tested during the 40 telephone interviews in Japan, 30 in Canada and 30 in the UK (giving a total of 100 interviews). One finding from the case studies was *not* supported by at least 50% of the telephone interviewees, namely only 46% of the interviewees agreed that a pension scheme had a major positive impact on their organisation's performance. However, 90% (27) of the Canadian interviewees agreed with this statement against 33% (13) of the Japanese and 20% (6) of the UK interviewees. The rising cost of funding final salary pension schemes was mentioned by some interviewees.

Only the Japanese interviewees were asked about their job for life policy with 88% (33) of these interviewees claiming that their organisation had a job for life policy. Of these 33 Japanese interviewees, 58% agreed that such a policy encouraged managers to take a long-term view but only 46% agreed that such a policy had a positive long-term effect on their organisation's performance. Furthermore, only 30% of these Japanese interviewees agreed that such a job for life policy increased the motivation of employees and only 45% agreed that such a policy increased loyalty from employees.

The following nine findings from the case studies were supported by 50% or more of the telephone interviewees:

1. A mix of financial and non-financial measures leads to improved organisational performance.

2. The role of employees is critical in achieving an organisation's targeted performance.

3. Teamwork has a major impact on an organisation's performance.

4. Organisational culture (with regard to employees) has a major impact on an organisation's performance.

5. When employees are viewed as assets rather than simply costs, this has a positive impact on an organisation's performance.

6. There is a positive link between training and an organisation's performance.

7. Benchmarking is a useful technique for exploring the relationship between HR policies and an organisation's performance.

8. Specific HR policies can be linked to an organisation's performance.

9. Statements could be made in an organisation's published report about the impact of HR policies on an organisation's performance.

Overall, in the researchers' opinion, it is difficult to link the effects of different HR policies with organisational performance because of both the time lags involved and the number of other factors affecting organisational performance. However, the case studies have shown that it is only by working in this area that our knowledge will improve.

## 4. Practical Implications

Three main findings from this research project are of particular interest to HR managers and management accountants. Firstly, the four HR policies mentioned by most interviewees in the six case studies as affecting organisational performance were:

a. recruitment

b. teamwork

c. organisational culture (with regard to employees)

d. training.

Secondly, management accountants provided information for and worked very closely with HR managers to support the HR management function to help improve organisational performance. In addition to the example below of exploring the links between HR policies and organisational performance, other examples included strategic plans and budgets (including variance analysis), performance-related bonus scheme and decision-making.

Thirdly, almost all the interviewees believed that HR policies affected organisational performance. Perhaps the most important finding is that in several of the case studies, management accountants and HR managers worked very closely together using benchmarking or employee surveys or a combination of both benchmarking and employee surveys to explore the links between HR policies and organisational performance.

Of the six case studies, Case F had made the greatest progress in establishing such links between specific HR policies and organisational performance. In the early 1990s, Case F entered into an HR benchmarking scheme with other organisations. The management accountants in Case F worked with HR managers to analyse the combined results (of the findings from the HR benchmarking scheme and the findings from its own annual surveys of employees' opinions) over several years to establish relationships between specific HR policies and organisational performance. Case F had to do this analysis over several years in order to overcome the twin problems of time lags (for example, between the introduction of a new HR policy and its resulting effect on organisational performance) and the number of other factors affecting organisational performance. It is important to emphasise that Case F used a specific HR benchmarking scheme as distinct from the external benchmarking used by some of the other cases. This breakthrough for Case F in linking the effects of specific HR policies to organisational performance was achieved by very close cooperation between its HR managers and management accountants.

# Introduction and Literature Review

## 1. Introduction

This research project examined the relationships between management accounting, human resource (HR) policies and organisational performance. Firstly, six case studies (two in Canada, two in Japan and two in the UK) were conducted and the researchers analysed the data collected to generate findings for each case. The cases covered building materials, consumer products, electronics, software development, timber products and a utility. Secondly, after all six cases were completed, the findings from these cases were compared in a cross-case analysis and the resulting 11 overall findings were then tested in 100 telephone interviews (30 in Canada, 40 in Japan and 30 in the UK).

The project built on the results of a previous project funded by CIMA on management accounting and strategic HR management (HRM) (Innes et al., 2001) by:

a. extending the research into the area of the relationship between different HR policies and organisational performance and, in particular, how management accountants help to establish links between HR policies and organisational performance;

b. extending the research into Japanese companies to give a different perspective and another point of comparison;

c. testing the case study results in a telephone survey.

The remainder of this opening chapter consists of a review of some relevant literature and a short discussion of the research approach used.

## 2. Literature Review

In November 2003 The Accounting for People Taskforce (established by the Secretary of State for Trade and Industry) published its final report on human capital management. Although the Taskforce concentrated on external financial reporting, it concluded that organisations should adopt human capital management as a driver of performance and attempt to measure it. Similarly, research by the Chartered Institute of Personnel and Development (2003) concluded that attempting to measure human capital will lead to better HRM policies and practices. This research by the Chartered Institute of Personnel and Development (2003) suggested that a correlation existed between the performance of companies and the ways in which they developed and managed people.

In 2002 CFO Research Services and Mercer Human Resource Consulting conducted a survey entitled 'Human Capital Management: The CFO's Perspective'. One finding of this survey was finance's changing approach to human capital with attempts being made to measure return on investment and to understand cause and effect relationships. Another finding from this survey was that 40% of the largest companies wished to measure the influence of human capital in relation to meeting business objectives. The report on this 2002 questionnaire survey concluded that as chief financial officers increasingly recognised the importance of human capital, they were beginning to seek better ways of measuring and managing this critical asset.

Bratton (1994, p. 5) defined strategic HRM as:

*that part of the management process that specialises in the management of people in work organisations. Human resource management emphasises that employees are the primary resource for gaining sustainable competitive advantage, that human resource activities need to be integrated with the corporate strategy, and that human resource specialists help organisational controllers to meet both efficiency and equity objectives.*

Some researchers have focused on HRM as strategic integration (Schuler and Jackson, 1987; Lengnick-Hall and Lengnick-Hall, 1988; Hendry and Pettigrew, 1990; Wright and McMahan, 1992). Hendry and Pettigrew (1986, p. 6) argued that 'human resource management has a role in creating competitive advantage in which the skills and motivation of a company's people and the way they are deployed can be a major source of competitive advantage'.

In a briefing document the Institute of Chartered Accountants in England and Wales (2003) quoted the Bath University research that tried to identify whether people management practices related to business outcomes. This research concluded that there were three series of people management actions related to motivation, ability and opportunity. The ICAEW (2003) roundtable discussion concluded that there was still a lack of evidence of a causal link between HRM policies and long-term organisational performance measures.

Stiles and Kulvisaechana (2003, p. 17) provided a review of the literature on human capital and organisational performance and concluded:

*We agree with Becker and Gerhart (1996, p. 786) who state that 'more effort should be devoted to finding out what managers are thinking when they make the decisions they do. This suggests a need for deeper qualitative research to complement the large scale, multiple firm studies that are available'.*

Berry and Bacon (2002) have conducted CIMA sponsored research into shareholder value perspectives and HRM. From interviews in FTSE 250 companies, Berry and Bacon (2002, p. 3) found that 'formal financial evaluation of HRM initiatives, either inside or outside the budgeting process, is virtually non-existent'. Bacon and Berry (2005, p. 6) concluded that 'identifying and demonstrating the link between HR and financial returns is very difficult'.

Some research studies have examined the relationship between HRM and organisational performance. Nkomo (1987) found no correlation between HR planning and business performance. Similarly, Delaney et al. (1989) reported no link between HR practices and financial performance. In contrast, Ulrich et al. (1984) found positive relationships between specific HR practices and business results. Schuler and Macmillan (1984, p. 242) suggested that 'effective management of human resources gives benefits which include greater profitability'. Gerhart and Milkovich (1992) found a link between training programmes and financial performance. Similarly, Bartel (1994) reported a link between training programmes and financial performance. Arthur (1994) collected data from 30 US steel mills and found that mills with commitment systems (in other words, developing committed employees to use their own discretion) had higher productivity, lower scrap rates and lower employee turnover than those with standard control systems.

Ichniowski et al. (1995) found that the use of HRM practices (such as work teams, flexible job assignments and training in multiple jobs) is associated with both high productivity and high financial performance in 65 business units. A study conducted by Huselid (1995) provided evidence that the use of HR practices (such as comprehensive recruitment and selection procedures, incentive compensation, performance management systems, extensive employee involvement and training) resulted in better organisational performance. Lengnick-Hall and Lengnick-Hall (1998, p. 468) concluded that 'organisations which engage in a strategy formulation process that systematically and reciprocally considers human resources and competitive strategy will perform better over the long term'.

Pfeffer (1998) found the need for consistency among seven HR practices to achieve effective performance with these seven HR practices being:

1. employment security,

2. selective hiring,

3. self-managed teams,

4. high compensation contingent on performance,

5. training,

6. reduction of status differentials,

7. sharing information.

In his exploratory study, Liao (2006, p. 716) concluded that 'empirical results from 93 firms reveal that the appropriate use of HRM control systems was a contributing factor to firm performance'. Kaya (2006, p. 2084) found that 'HRM practices (which emphasise behaviour and attitude, extensive training on job skills, written instructions and procedures, team activities, training in multiple functions, incentive to meet objectives, communication of strategy, interaction facilities and feedback on performance) are important for enhancing firm performance'.

Such research studies provide evidence of a link between HRM and organisational performance. However, to date most of this research has been conducted by HRM specialists rather than management accountants. Management accounting is one way of reporting the HRM–organisational performance link. Purcell (1995, p. 84) argued that 'the challenge of human resource management is to show a link between policy, practice, and organisational outcomes that is meaningful to the corporate board'. That is a role for management accounting. Armstrong (1995) has suggested that the outcome (performance) of HRM activities can be reported in management accounting terms. Ezzamel et al. (1995) suggested that achieving a competitive advantage through strategic HRM placed an increased emphasis on the need for organisations to take a more strategic approach to managing their employees. Some Japanese organisations had a more direct link between corporate strategies and management accounting compared to Western organisations. For example, Hiromoto (1988) argued that Japanese organisations used their accounting system to motivate employees in more of an 'influencing role' than an 'information role' in the managerial process.

## 3.  Research Approach

Yin (1994, p. 13) defined the case study method as 'an empirical inquiry that investigates a contemporary phenomenon within its real-life context when the boundaries between phenomenon and context are not clearly evident; and in which multiple sources of evidence are used'. Yin (1994) referred to a case study as investigating a 'contemporary phenomenon' or a particular issue but, in this report, the term 'case study' referred to one organisation. The six case studies in this research project included a site tour, observation, examination of relevant documents and seven interviews in each case with at least two management accountants, at least two HR managers and at least two managers with special responsibility for some aspect of organisational performance. Two researchers were present during all six cases. On average the interviewees had at least 10 years of experience in all the cases.

Spicer (1992) suggested that multiple case studies allow the data to be analysed and compared to identify similarities and differences that provide the basis for building theory. There is no perfect number of case studies, but Eisenhardt

(1989, p. 545) suggested that 'a number between 4 and 10 cases usually works well'. This research project had six cases. The researchers started each case with an open mind but not an empty mind (having knowledge of the literature) to ensure the collection of sufficient and relevant data (Dey, 1993). The researchers used semi-structured interviews asking broad questions to allow the interviewees to talk openly about the topic and to try to ensure that the researchers did not influence the interviewees' responses. The researchers then asked follow-up questions such as 'can you explain this in more detail', 'can you give an example', 'why' or 'how' to allow the research topic to be explored in more depth.

Coding procedures were used to analyse the data collected from each case to determine the findings from each case. A full draft write-up of each case (including these findings) was given to each organisation for their comments and in order to correct any factual inaccuracies. After all six cases had been completed, the researchers did a cross-case analysis to identify similarities between the findings (from the six individual cases) that could be developed into overall findings. A similar finding from at least three cases was developed into an overall finding. Eleven overall findings emerged from this cross-case analysis to be tested during the telephone interviews in Canada, Japan and the UK.

The researchers converted these 11 overall findings into draft questions for the telephone interviews and these draft questions were pilot tested with six management accountants. After this pilot test, the researchers amended these draft questions for the final questionnaire. It was decided to use phone interviews rather than a postal questionnaire. A random sample was taken from the top 1,000 companies in Canada, Japan and the UK. The phone interviewees in the companies selected were finance directors or management accountants. If a company did not wish to participate in this telephone survey, the next company in the sample was selected until 40 phone interviews were conducted in Japan, 30 in Canada and 30 in the UK to give a total of 100 telephone interviews.

Chapters 2–7 present the results of the six case studies. Chapter 8 reports the analysis of the results from the cross-case analysis and from the 100 telephone interviews. Chapter 9 has the conclusions from the six case studies and 100 telephone interviews.

# Case A

## 1. Research Site

Case A is a Japanese multinational company in the manufacturing sector and has been established for almost 100 years. Case A was listed on the Tokyo Stock Exchange. There were more than 100,000 employees in the whole organisation and approximately 1,500 employees at the research site. The turnover for the entire organisation was more than £10,000 million. The total employee costs (including pension costs) were approximately 30% of total costs.

At this research site there were 20 finance staff and most of these were management accountants. There were 10 HR staff members at this research site. Generally the interviewees considered the competition for employees for this research site to be extremely intense (that is, 7 on a scale of 1 to 7).

## 2. Interviewees

There were seven interviewees, three being management accountants, two HR managers and two other managers (in engineering and marketing). All interviewees had a first degree and their experience in their current field of expertise ranged from 10 to 25 years with an average of more than 15 years. All the interviewees had worked for Case A since their university graduation. In addition to interviews and observation, interviewees provided copies of a number of documents.

## 3. HR Policies

The interviewees (ranging from 30 to 60 years of age) in Case A were examples of the 'job for life' policy that still exists in large Japanese multinational companies, although, in recent years, this policy has come under increasing pressure. Given this 'job for life' policy, the interviewees considered themselves as, firstly, Case A employees and, secondly, as management accountants, HR managers and other functional managers. All seven interviewees had experienced the normal training programme of working in several different functional areas of the business before taking up their current posts. The interviewees identified primarily with Case A rather than with their functional specialism. It also meant that the interviewees had a very wide knowledge about the business of Case A, and also the interviewees had a very large range of contacts (throughout Case A) with whom they had worked in the past.

This 'job for life' policy had implications for recruitment and training. Interviewees considered that the recruitment of the correct mix of employees has an important positive impact on organisational performance. Obviously the recruitment decision of each employee had major long-term implications for Case A. Recruitment is very much a capital investment decision involving well over £1 million of salary costs per employee over their working lives. Training becomes a top priority with a long-term view taken. Indeed the interviewees talked not about training but about internal education.

# 4.   Findings

## 4.1.   Performance Measurement

Performance was defined in Case A by a mix of financial and non-financial measures. Financial measures were predominant with close monitoring of sales (including sales per employee), costs and number of employees. Employees were also paid a bonus depending on actual profit performance against budget, and so bonus accounting was an area of discussion between HR managers and management accountants.

The financial performance model used to assess divisions was a weighted average model as follows:

| | |
|---|---|
| Achievement of budget | 25% |
| Cash flow | 20% |
| Profitability | 15% |
| Improvement | 15% |
| Non-financial measures | 15% |
| Growth | 10% |
| | 100% |

Achievement of budget has the highest rating followed by cash flow. Case A reviewed its budget every six months. The interviewees considered this performance model as an influential tool in relation to the performance of divisions but much less influential in relation to the performance of individual employees. On the basis of this performance model, divisions were rated on a scale A, B and B+. The divisional rating then determined the level of bonus for individuals within that particular division. Generally, the interviewees were not happy with the weightings used in the above performance model.

Although the non-financial measures were weighted only 15% in the perform-ance model, the HR managers considered the non-financial performance measures to be much more important than just 15%. For example, five years ago an annual survey of employees' opinions was started and the results have become very influ-ential in Case A. Indeed, interviewees considered that the two most important critical success factors for Case A were, firstly, the quality of its employees and, secondly, its competitive engineering position. Interviewees suggested that using a mix of financial and non-financial measures helped to improve overall organisa-tional performance.

## 4.2.  Employees

All interviewees considered the role of employees in achieving Case A's budgeted performance to be extremely important, namely seven on a scale of 1 (not impor-tant at all) to 7 (extremely important). Employees within Case A were regarded as 'assets' who created additional value rather than 'costs' that the organisation had to recover. Again the 'job for life' policy was mentioned when interviewees talked about employees as 'assets'. Generally employees could not be made redundant although, in 2002, Case A had introduced an early retirement scheme.

## 4.3.  Links between Management Accountants and HR Managers

Interviewees regarded the performance-related bonus scheme as one important topic of communication between management accountants and HR managers in relation to performance measurement. For example, management accountants discussed the financial and non-financial components of the bonus model with HR manag-ers before the proposed model was finalised and then later interpreted the actual results from the bonus scheme. However, the most critical link between manage-ment accountants and HR managers was in relation to the plan for the next three years that was developed from Case A's vision and budget. A key component of this plan (and the resulting annual budgets) was the proposed number of employees. This number of employees was linked explicitly to the level of output expected by Case A. The basic assumption was that the existing employees would learn any new skills that Case A required. The salary levels were estimated by HR managers and fed into the annual budget.

In Case A there is a monthly meeting between HR managers and management accountants with the emphasis of the discussion being on non-financial perform-ance measures. However, the management accountants also discussed comparison of monthly actual results against budget with both HR and other managers. Another area for discussion between HR managers, other managers and management accountants was the training budget that was set using two main criteria, namely:

1. past experience and
2. future skill requirements.

As one interviewee stated:

> *It is basically our belief that our training expenditure leads to an improvement in organisational performance. Remember that with our jobs for life policy, it is critical that our existing employees develop the new skills required for the future success of Case A. Training is therefore at least as important as any capital expenditure. Training is critical for the future success of this organisation.*

When asked how Case A measured the overall value added by employees, most interviewees said that Case A trusted employees to add value to the organisation. Indeed most interviewees considered that the employees contributed the greatest percentage of Case A's value added.

## 4.4.   HR Policies and Organisational Performance

With the 'job for life' policy, very close control was exercised over the number of new employees recruited. Furthermore, a lot of emphasis was placed on 'hiring internally'. Three years ago the policy of an internal free agent system was introduced. Theoretically this meant that any employee could apply for any job in any division, although in practice limits were imposed. Although the 'job for life' policy had been reviewed because of the increased competitive pressure faced by Case A, it had survived this review. All the interviewees considered that this 'job for life' policy had a profound effect on Case A's performance. All the interviewees considered that the motivation of employees was extremely high. The social status of employees depended on the success of Case A. Every employee wanted to see Case A prosper in the long term. The 'job for life' policy led not only to great employee motivation but also to intense organisational loyalty from employees.

Interviewees believed that the 'job for life' policy encouraged all employees to take the long-term view and avoid trying to improve organisational performance in the short term by, for example, reducing training costs. Indeed one manager said that:

> *When we went through a very difficult financial period a few years ago, we decided to increase our training budget because we realised that we needed our employees to develop some new skills necessary for Case A's survival.*

*Remember that we are training very loyal and very motivated employees. In fact, to fund such training investment in the past, all employees in Case A agreed to take a small salary reduction.*

Several interviewees considered that the improving financial position of Case A was directly linked to this specific increase in training a few years ago and indirectly to the 'job for life' policy. Case A had an Education Division that provided training to employees throughout the group and also a subsidiary, the Education Academy, that:

1. educated new employees (both graduates and non-graduates),
2. provided management level education similar to an MBA education and
3. provided specialist education in areas such as information technology and the law.

Last year Case A changed its salary policy. Previously all employees were categorised one to five in relation to a salary scale. However, a few years ago a system of management by objectives was introduced coupled with a feedback system. Case A was monitoring the effects of this change in policy in relation to organisational performance. The results were very tentative but the initial findings were that younger staff preferred the new system. Some interviewees suggested that younger staff were fairly doubtful about the 'job for life' policy surviving long into the future and would therefore prefer salary and promotion to be linked more directly to individual performance and less to age and seniority. In particular, information technology staff much preferred the new management by objectives system because of the contribution made by younger staff in the area of information technology. The interviewees suggested that the performance-related bonus scheme had helped to improve Case A's performance.

One way that Case A was attempting to assess this particular change in HR policy was by surveying employees for their views. By comparing the results of such employee surveys over a number of years, Case A was trying to link the introduction of specific HR policies with organisational performance. Interviewees accepted that such a link was difficult to establish with any certainty. However, generally, interviewees considered that by attempting to make an explicit link between a new HR policy and organisational performance, Case A was becoming better at assessing the effects of the introduction of new HR policies. It was still very much an inexact science but as one interviewee said:

*It is only by attempting to link HR policies and organisational performance that we will improve our expertise in this area.*

## 4.5.   External Reporting

Most interviewees considered that HRM and organisational performance information could be reported better both internally to managers and externally to shareholders and other stakeholders. Although some of this information would be quantitative (such as number of employees) and monetary (such as investment in training), most of such information would be qualitative (such as a description of the 'job for life' policy and a summary of new skills developed by existing employees). Most interviewees considered that it would be very difficult to link specific HR policies with improved organisational performance in monetary terms. However, most interviewees considered that qualitative statements could be made in terms of top management's view of the HR policy's impact on organisational performance. Interviewees thought that such qualitative statements would interest at least some stakeholders.

## 5.   Summary

The following findings emerged from Case A:

1.  A 'job for life' policy for employees has several implications including the following:
    a.   New skills are developed by existing employees.
    b.   A long-term view is encouraged.
    c.   There is a positive impact on organisational performance.
    d.   Employee motivation is increased.
    e.   Organisational loyalty from employees is increased.
2.  If employees are not happy with the weightings used in a performance model, this will have an adverse effect on organisational performance.
3.  A mix of financial and non-financial measures helps to improve overall organisational performance.
4.  A performance-related bonus scheme helps to improve organisational performance.
5.  Recruitment of the correct mix of employees has a positive impact on organisational performance.
6.  Budgets and strategic plans are significant communication links between management accountants and HR managers.
7.  When employees are viewed as assets (rather than costs), this has a positive impact on organisational performance.

8. The training budget is set using two main criteria, namely past experience and future skill requirements.

9. There is a positive link (with a time lag) between well-planned training (both for new and existing employees) and improved organisational performance.

10. Employee surveys over a number of years are one way of linking the introduction of specific HR policies with organisational performance.

11. It is difficult to link specific HR policies with improved organisational performance in monetary terms.

12. In an annual report, qualitative statements could be made in terms of top management's view of an HR policy's impact on organisational performance.

# Case B

## 1. Research Site

Case B is a Japanese company in the manufacturing sector and has been established for almost 100 years. Case B was listed on the Tokyo Stock Exchange. There were more than 25,000 employees in the whole organisation and approximately 2,000 employees at this research site. The turnover for the entire organisation was more than £5,000 million. The total employee costs were approximately 30% of total costs.

At the research site there were 40 finance staff and half of these were management accountants. There were 15 HR members of staff at this research site. Generally the interviewees considered the competition for employees for this research site to be of moderate intensity (that is, 4 on a scale of 1 to 7).

## 2. Interviewees

There were seven interviewees, three being management accountants, two HR managers and two other managers (marketing and purchasing). All seven interviewees had a first degree and their experience in their current field of expertise ranged from 10 to 30 years with an average of more than 15 years. All seven of the interviewees had worked for Case B since their university graduation. In addition to interviews and observation, interviewees provided copies of a number of documents.

## 3. HR Policies

Case B had a 'job for life' policy. Most employees in Case B were graduates who had joined the company straight from university and worked all their life to date in Case B and expected to work for it until their retirement. The interviewees suggested that this 'job for life' policy was coming under pressure from international competition and other factors but it was still a major influence on Case B's organisational performance. The employees in Case B regarded themselves as, firstly, Case B employees and, secondly, as HR managers, other functional managers and management accountants. All the interviewees had experienced the standard training programme of working in several different functional areas of the business before taking up their current posts.

With this 'job for life' policy, Case B took great care with its recruitment and training programmes because of the long-term implications. Training programmes were used to develop new skills for existing employees. The interviewees considered that this 'job for life' policy encouraged all employees to take a long-term view and this approach had a beneficial effect on Case B's overall performance. The interviewees considered that this 'job for life' policy meant that employees really identified with Case B and this increased employee loyalty and motivation.

In recent years, Case B introduced a performance-related bonus system based on a form of Economic Value Added (EVA) (registered trademark of Stern Stewart & Co.). This system used both company targets and individual performance targets. When individual employees were not meeting their targets, they were given assistance to improve their performance including additional training if necessary. Every employee worked towards special targets derived from Case B's overall targets. These individual targets were defined as 'stretched goals' that challenged employees. The bonus for individual employees depended on how well they met their individual targets. Part of the bonus for employees also depended on how well Case B met its own overall targets. The interviewees considered this bonus scheme helped to improve organisational performance.

## 4.   Findings

### 4.1.   Performance Measurement

Case B used a form of EVA being net operating profit after tax less a charge for the cost of capital employed. Case B had a five-year plan with new EVA goals being set every year and adjustments made every six months. The interviewees confirmed that 'sustainable growth' was the fundamental goal of Case B. The performance targets were mostly set by top management but there was some negotiation on individual targets for employees. In addition, managers provided forecasts that were fed into the budget process.

In addition to EVA, Case B used cash flow as a performance measure and a number of non-financial measures. The non-financial measures included the following:

1.  customer satisfaction,
2.  employee morale,
3.  quality,
4.  market share,
5.  safety,

6. environmental protection and

7. social contribution.

The interviews suggested that the social contribution performance measure was becoming increasingly important. Under safety, Case B had reduced the number of employees involved in industrial accidents by more than 50% over a two-year period.

The interviews considered that the use of a mix of financial and non-financial performance measures helped to improve the overall performance of Case B. Efforts were being made to link the above non-financial performance measures with the future financial performance of Case B but these efforts were at a fairly early stage of development. However, Case B was going to continue these efforts – in particular, to try to clarify the time lag between improvements in the non-financial measures resulting in improvements in the financial measures. The interviewees had no doubt about the relationship between non-financial and financial performance measures.

Case B benchmarked its performance both between business units within its own organisations and against other organisations including its competitors. The interviewees confirmed that Case B had identified a number of key performance indicators (both financial and non-financial as identified above) and tried to benchmark these indicators both internally and externally. The interviewees considered that the information resulting from benchmarking HR information helped to improve the overall performance of Case B. Case B placed as much emphasis on internal benchmarking as on external benchmarking to improve its overall performance.

## 4.2.  Employees

All interviewees considered employees to be 'assets' rather than costs. The interviewees had no doubt that the quality of employees was the most critical success factor for Case B. With the 'job for life' policy, hiring new employees was a major decision and the training of new employees was also critical. As one interviewee said:

> *Hiring a new employee is similar to a capital investment decision for a new machine of well over £1 million. In addition, if we do not like the machine we can always sell it but we have a new graduate for 40 years.*

New employees had a formal and structured training programme but there was also on-the-job training. This included new employees spending a number of years in different functional job such as production, purchasing and sales. Several interviewees referred to 'life-time training' for all employees.

Another aspect mentioned by most interviewees was the importance of teamwork. The interviewees considered that teamwork had a major positive influence on Case B's overall performance. The interviewees suggested that teamwork came naturally to most Japanese employees who liked to belong to a group. Furthermore, the status of employees outside Case B depended mainly on the image of Case B in Japanese society.

The interviewees accepted that the 'job for life' policy, the 'life-time training' and viewing employees as 'assets' all led to increased costs but the interviewees considered that the resulting improved organisational performance more than compensated for these increased costs. The interviewees agreed that in the short term increased costs could outweigh the benefits but in the long term the benefits were several times greater than the costs.

## 4.3.    Links between Management Accountants and HR Managers

The bonus system based on a form of EVA was an important link between management accountants, HR managers and other functional managers. The management accountants interpreted the meaning of EVA reports for HR and other managers. As well as organisational targets, individual employees had targets linked to EVA. Managers held meetings with employees who were not achieving their targets and, therefore, it was important that everyone understood the meaning of EVA. The management accountants reported a breakdown of EVA on a monthly basis to all employees.

The detailed budget was another important communication link between management accountants, HR managers and other functional managers. The functional managers, HR managers and management accountants worked closely together in relation to the HR budget – for example, the total number of employees to be included in next year's budget and, in particular, the number of graduates to be recruited next year. Another example was a long-term training programme that was the basis for the annual training budget. The training budget was the outcome of extensive discussions between functional managers, HR managers and management accountants. The HR managers and management accountants also had close communication (formal reports, formal meetings and informal discussions) about the actual results against the budget.

## 4.4.    HR Policies and Organisational Performance

The interviewees considered that the 'job for life' was the most important HR policy affecting Case B's organisational performance. With its 'job for life' policy, the HR managers and management accountants spent a lot of time discussing the necessary number and mix of employees because recruiting each new employee was such a big long-term decision. The interviewees had no doubt that their 'job for life' policy and their recruitment policy had positive long-term effects on Case B's organisational performance. One interviewee suggested that 'our job for life policy is the framework for our success because it means that employees are not only motivated but also dedicated to Case B. Case B is the first priority for our employees and they will do whatever they can to ensure that Case B is as successful as possible'. Another interviewee emphasised that 'our job for life policy ensures that we can take a long-term view when making decisions because we know that we are going to live with the consequences of these decisions'.

Over the last few years Case B had improved its performance. Although interviewees considered that managers took the long-term view when making decisions, there were quarterly reviews of targets to check progress and there was follow-up to ensure that future targets would be met. As one interviewee said 'we take a long-term view but we do not neglect the short-term targets'.

Although the interviewees considered that the 'job for life' was the most important HR policy affecting organisational performance, they also mentioned a number of other policies with positive effects on organisational performance. Firstly, there was teamwork. All the interviewees emphasised the importance of teamwork for Case B at all levels of the organisation. The interviewees considered teamwork to be the second most important HR influence on Case B's organisational performance after the 'job for life' policy.

Secondly, there was the commitment of employees in Case B. Thirdly, the interviewees considered that the long-term training for employees improved Case B's organisational performance. The interviewees suggested that training for employees was the third most important HR influence on Case B's organisational performance. Several interviewees mentioned that increasing the knowledge and skills of employees led to increased customer satisfaction that in turn led to improved organisational performance. One interviewee commented that 'our improved results can be attributed to the teamwork, commitment and training of our employees who had enabled us to overcome challenges in all areas of our business'.

## 4.5.   External Reporting

Most interviewees considered that Case B's HR policies and organisational performance could be disclosed externally but the statements would be mainly qualitative rather quantitative. For example, the 'job for life' policy could be disclosed but the interviewees considered that it would be impossible to state much more than this policy had a positive long-term effect on Case B's organisational performance. The interviewees suggested that the other HR policies such as teamwork and training could also be disclosed with qualitative (and possibly some quantitative) statements about the effects of these policies on Case B's organisational performance.

# 5. Summary

The following findings emerged from Case B:

1. A 'job for life' policy has a positive effect on organisational performance.
2. A 'job for life' policy encourages managers to take the long-term view when making decisions.
3. A 'job for life' policy increases the commitment of employees to an organisation.
4. A 'job for life' policy increases employee loyalty and motivation.
5. The use of a mix of financial and non-financial performance measures helps to improve overall organisational performance.
6. A performance-related bonus scheme helps to improve organisational performance.
7. Benchmarking results can help to show the relationship between specific HR policies and organisational performance.
8. Recruitment of the correct number and mix of employees has a positive long-term effect on organisational performance.
9. Teamwork can have a positive impact on organisational performance.
10. 'Life-time training' can have a positive effect on organisational performance.
11. Viewing employees as 'assets' rather than costs has a positive impact on organisational performance.
12. A performance-related bonus scheme is an important channel of communication between HR managers and managements accountants.
13. The annual budget is an important channel of communication between HR managers and management accountants.
14. Management accountants can interpret the meaning of EVA reports for HR and other managers.
15. Qualitative and quantitative statements could be made in the annual report about HR policies and their impact on organisational performance.

# Case C

## 1. Research Site

Case C is a multinational manufacturing company that has been operating in Canada for about 100 years. There were more than 10,000 employees in the entire organisation, and at the research sites (plant and head office) there were approximately 1,000 employees although a few years ago this number was much larger. At the plant approximately two-thirds of the employees were hourly paid and the remaining one-third was salaried. The turnover for the entire organisation was over £5,000 million. The total employee costs (including pension costs) were approximately 35% of total costs.

At the research sites there were 15 finance staff, approximately half of whom were management accountants. There were five HR members of staff at the research sites. Generally the interviewees considered the competition for employees at the research sites to be extremely competitive (that is, 7 on a scale of 1 to 7).

## 2. Interviewees

Interviews were conducted at one plant and at the Canadian head office. There were seven interviewees, two being management accountants, two HR managers and three other managers (in manufacturing). All interviewees were graduates and had more than 10 years' working experience and had been employed by Case C for between 5 and 25 years. Each interview lasted for more than an hour and, in addition to the interviews and observation, the interviewees provided copies of a number of documents.

## 3. HR Policies

Case C had a big initiative on training. Existing employees were trained to develop new skills involving hundreds of thousands of hours of training throughout the organisation. Training firms were employed and ran workshops so that employees could become multi-skilled. Workshops were also run on soft skills and leadership. In addition to 'classroom training', there was a lot of on-the-job training. Case C operated a training contract process for all applications for training courses. This training contract included a 'transfer of learning' plan where employees explained how they were going to transfer their new learning to their daily functional role after the training course was completed.

In the recent past, Case C had 'downsized' and a number of employees had to be made redundant. The multi-skills of employees had helped Case C after this downsizing because the remaining employees were usually able to do the jobs of those made redundant. Case C had a strong union covering all of its employees and worked with this union during this 'downsizing'. For example, in the whole of Case C there were more than 2,000 employees with more than 30 years' service and they were offered an attractive, voluntary, early retirement package. However, even after this 'downsizing', the interviewees considered that recruiting the right quality and mix of employees was critical to Case C's performance.

Case C centralised its HR function for all of North America in one location where the transactional aspects of HRM were processed with the line supervisor providing the input electronically. Basically the HR offices were moved out of the plants into a centralised operation. As one HR interviewee said:

*You could say that the centralised HR operates at the very highest strategic level and the very lowest transactional level.*

In addition there were HR area managers that supported an area including manufacturing plants and distribution centres. Problems with this centralised HR function had to be solved such as the Privacy Act in Canada regarding the records of individual employees. Recently this centralised HR function had developed a retirement profile to identify losses of significant employees and key knowledge loss so that such gaps could be filled in a timely manner. A method had been developed to capture and retain such knowledge that included a detailed succession plan. Similarly there was a programme to develop and retain key individuals. Case C had an 'organisation and human resources review' to support and develop employees.

In the past, managers in this group moved every two or three years. Now there was a great push on group practices and policies. The group was trying to change its culture and the current programme was 'leader for tomorrow' involving more employee empowerment. The 'leader for tomorrow' programme was a participative process of continuous improvement involving all employees that aimed to develop a performance culture. The leadership profile included the following:

1. vision and purpose (including interpreting and applying the business vision to meet local needs),
2. driving for results (including understanding the drivers underlying the key performance indicators and using people development to improve results),

3. customer focus (including establishing business processes for both internal and external customers),

4. leading change (including an ability to manage the human aspects of change initiatives) and

5. integrity and values (including managing a team so that the behaviour was consistent with Case C's values).

The interviewees considered that Case C's changing organisational culture (including the above 'leader for tomorrow' programme) had a big positive impact on its performance.

# 4.  Findings

## 4.1.  Performance Measurement

For Case C, benchmarking against other plants within the group and against competitors was very important. The management accountants interpreted some of the benchmarking information for HR managers. In terms of benchmarking within the group, the level of fixed costs was critical as were quality, customer satisfaction and employee productivity. Productivity was measured in terms of physical output per man hour. The main financial performance measure used for benchmarking against competitors was cost per ton. Safety was another important area of performance and measures included lost time in days and number of medical incidents per 200,000 hours. The interviewees considered that benchmarking was a useful technique for exploring the relationships between HR policies and Case C's overall performance over a number of years – for example, by tracing the effects of a new (or changed) HR policy in one year with future organisational performance. Such tracing was an imprecise science because of the number of other factors affecting organisational performance and because of time lags but the interviewees said that, with experience, some interesting links between a new (or changed) HR policy and organisational performance began to emerge from such benchmarking (particularly from the benchmarking within the group where only one plant introduced a new or changed HR policy).

The interviewees talked about a quadruple bottom line with a particular emphasis on the environmental aspect. Environmental measures included the amount of by-product for landfill. Case C had to operate within its environmental permits and constraints. Case C also measured its unit power consumption and power efficiency.

Overall there were 15 key performance indicators that were used in the bonus system and financial measures accounted for only three of these 15 indicators. The interviewees suggested that this mix of non-financial and financial indicators helped to improve organisational performance. The main financial performance measurement was Economic Value Added (EVA) (registered trademark of Stern Stewart). Indeed the bonus scheme for managers was split 50% each between personal objectives and EVA. Individual employee performance targets were linked directly to the organisation's goals and key performance targets. Case C had three phases in its performance management system. The first phase was performance planning that included reviewing business unit objectives and key performance indicators, setting personal objectives for the year and planning development action. The second phase was performance coaching and interim review that included tracking process, addressing any problems and adjusting objectives if necessary. The third phase was performance reviewing that included reviewing results of personal objectives, discussing new development plan and discussing new objectives.

## 4.2. Employees

All interviewees considered employees to be 'assets' rather than costs. For example, various interviewees said the following:

*People are the key to our success.*

*A good individual can have a tremendous impact.*

*When you get individuals who have good, strong interpersonal management skills, people working for them are more satisfied, more motivated and there are fewer problems in the plant.*

*We are fortunate that we have highly skilled trades people in this plant with a good strong work ethic and that is the reason that the plant performs well.*

*When you lose a key person, your plant can stop progressing.*

Most of the interviewees emphasised that a good pension scheme motivated employees to improve organisational performance. The interviewees considered that viewing employees as 'assets' led to increased costs in the short run (such as training) but better organisational performance in the long run.

## 4.3. Links between Management Accountants and HR Managers

The annual budget was one link between management accountants and HR managers. In particular, the interviewees mentioned the training budget. Case C has placed a great deal of emphasis on training with the ultimate objective of reducing the cost per ton of production.

Another example of the link between management accountants and HR managers was 'workers' compensation payments'. The management accountants calculated that, as a percentage of total costs, Case C spent four times as much on workers' compensation as its competitors in the same industry. The HR managers and management accountants were now working together and had already managed to reduce very significantly Case C's workers' compensation payments. The downsizing period had been another time when the management accountants and the HR managers had worked very closely together. Indeed after the downsizing and the training, the employees set improved records for both levels of production and quality.

The management accountants and the HR managers worked closely together not only in relation to the training budget and training costs but also in relation to the HRM budget and costs. Over recent years a critical decision for the future of this plant was the total number of employees for the coming year and the necessary mix of skills within the workforce. Another link between the management accountants and the HR managers was the bonus scheme involving a mix of 15 financial and non-financial performance measures. The management accountants interpreted the meaning of EVA for HR and other managers. There were monthly meetings between the management accountants and the HR managers to discuss the actual results.

The management cycle within Case C to achieve greater organisational efficiency consisted of four phases. They are as follows:

1. strategic review to examine medium-term strategy,
2. action plan for performance improvement over two or three years,
3. the above organisational and HRs review and
4. a budget that evolved to take account of other elements of this management cycle.

This management cycle provided another link (particularly the third and fourth phases) between management accountants and HR managers.

## 4.4. HR Policies and Organisational Performance

The training programme at this particular plant has been identified by Case C as best practice for the entire worldwide group. Case C managers from countries such as Brazil, France and the USA (as well as from other Canadian plants) had visited the plant to study particularly its supervisory training programme. The plant had consolidated all the managers' individual training budgets and, with one consolidated training budget, had adopted a zero-based budgeting approach to ensure that 'important developmental training took place rather than just training for training's sake'.

The plant-wide training plan meant that each employee had a personal developmental training contract. The interviewees claimed that such an approach to training not only controlled the training costs (particularly by eliminating unnecessary training) but also ensured that training fitted with the plant's developmental plan. This plant also tried to link the output from its training to its organisational performance. It did this in two ways. Firstly, it had a list of required skills for the future operation of the plant and monitored such skills with the skills emerging from its training programme giving it a macro-approach to linking its training to its organisational performance. Secondly, it adopted a micro-approach requiring all employees to write a report both 30 days and 90 days after the completion of their training programme. The reports analysed how well that specific training programme met that particular employee's own personal development training contract.

Most of the interviewees emphasised how the changing culture of Case C helped it to improve its organisational performance. Case C was changing its culture with an empowerment programme for employees and this programme had led to an increase in the number of suggestions made by employees. One example was that the suggestions led directly to an improvement in both the quality and reliability of Case C's products. This was important because two of Case C's critical success factors were better quality and better reliability than its competitors.

The interviewees also considered that Case C's performance appraisal system had helped to improve its organisational performance. Interviewees mentioned both the formal appraisal system for all employees (including hourly paid employees) that identified training development opportunities and the informal appraisal system. The interviewees considered the informal appraisal system to be an important factor in improving organisational performance because the formal appraisals generally took place only once a year but the informal appraisal and feedback for all employees were an ongoing process throughout the year. The interviewees suggested that these informal appraisals had more impact on organisational performance than the formal appraisals.

However, the main HR policy that emerged from Case C was its training and all the interviewees were certain that Case C's training programme had improved Case C's organisational performance over the long term. In particular, the interviewees emphasised the importance of training in helping Case C to emerge as a very successful business after its downsizing period.

## 4.5.    External Reporting

The interviewees considered that Case C's HR policies could be disclosed externally but the links to organisational performance would be mainly qualitative statements. For example, the training programme could be disclosed in some detail. Examples could be given from the 30-day and 60-day reports of how this training programme had improved individual performance and then summarised information could be given about how the training programme had improved organisational performance. However, the interviewees mentioned the problem of the time lag but again suggested that a mix of examples and qualitative statements could be disclosed.

## 5. Summary

The following findings emerged from Case C:

1. Training before, during and after a downsizing period can lead to improved organisational performance.

2. Recruiting the right quality and mix of employees is critical for future organisational performance.

3. Much of the HR function (both at the strategic and transactional levels) can be centralised in one location for each country to improve organisational performance.

4. A change in organisational culture can lead to improved organisational performance.

5. Management accountants can interpret benchmarking information (both within the group and against competitors) for HR managers.

6. Benchmarking is a useful technique for exploring the relationships between HR policies and organisational performance.

7. A performance-related bonus scheme can improve organisational performance.

8. A good pension scheme can lead to improved organisational performance.

9. Considering employees as assets (rather than costs) can lead to increased costs in the short term but to improved organisational performance in the long term.

10. A bonus scheme is an important communication link between management accountants and HR managers.

11. An organisational and HR review that ties into the budget is an important link between management accountants and managers.

12. Informal appraisals can improve organisational performance at least as much as formal appraisals.

13. The annual report could include qualitative statements about the links between certain HR policies and organisational performance.

# Case D

## 1. Research Site

Case D is a private Canadian company in the timber products sector and it started trading in the beginning of the twentieth century. Case D had more than 5,000 employees in the whole organisation and approximately 300 employees at this research site. The turnover for the entire organisation was more than £1,000 million with sales in more than 20 countries. The total employee costs were approximately 30% of total costs.

At the research site there were five finance members of staff with two management accounting staff. There were two HR members of staff at this research site and five HR managers at the head office. Generally the interviewees considered the competition for employees for this research site to be extremely intense (that is, 7 on a scale of 1 to 7).

## 2. Interviewees

There were seven interviewees, two being management accounting staff, two HR members of staff (one at the research site and one at head office) and three other managers (maintenance, production and the plant manager who also had a management accounting background). All interviewees had a first degree and their experience in their current field of expertise ranged from 10 to 35 years with an average of more than 15 years. Six of the seven interviewees had worked for Case D for more than 20 years which was not unusual at this site with many employees being long-serving (that is, with more than 20 years' service). In addition to the interviews and observation, interviewees provided copies of a number of documents.

## 3. HR Policies

Case D had four values (in its vision statement and mentioned by interviewees) that affected particularly its HR policies. The first value was respect for people as the foundation of all its business practices. This respect for people was demonstrated through its 'commitment to safety, the environment and internal and external business relationships'. The second value was progressiveness with all staff being encouraged to propose new ideas and take ownership of their work with individual initiative and innovation being valued. A third value was integrity requiring all employees to be honest, fair and ethical. The fourth value was open communication to enhance job satisfaction and performance.

Case D had a biannual employee opinion survey and focus groups throughout the organisation and feedback from these two sources influenced Case D's HR policies. Furthermore, employee opinion surveys helped to show the relationship between specific HR policies and organisational performance. Following the takeover of another company in 2005, one focus in 2006 was on organisational development and employee engagement. Recently, Case D had started a Leadership Survey to allow employees to provide confidential feedback on their supervisors' leadership effectiveness.

There was a group performance and appraisal process to support the development of all employees. Case D had a group system that produced statistics on employees and also tracked HR initiatives. In recent years Case D had improved its pension scheme and most of the interviewees considered that Case D now had one of the best company pension schemes in Canada.

Interestingly, the plant was recognised in the group as having the best practices for hiring and developing employees. This plant used the group HR tests such as specific skills tests (for example, electrical and mechanical skills) and personality tests but did the hiring without any other HR assistance. The view taken was that the managers understood best the knowledge and skills required for any post and, as importantly, whether a particular individual would fit into the culture of the team and, therefore, were the best people to do the interviewing and make the hiring decision without any other HR input. The interviewees all agreed that this hiring approach had been extremely successful as measured by the plant's operational and financial performance and its very low employee turnover during the past five years.

Another HR policy adopted by the managers in the plant was a very specific type of training on the job which involved identifying the knowledge required for specific jobs, giving a list of questions to employees to help them identify for themselves where there was a knowledge gap. The employees themselves then took the necessary steps (including training courses) to bridge their knowledge gap. A linked policy was, where possible, to promote employees from within the organisation.

In addition to the emphasis on training, Case D placed a lot of emphasis on communication. The basic belief was that people value communication and the management style was to work together with very open communication within the plant.

# 4.   Findings

## 4.1.   Performance Measurement

Case D defined performance in terms of a mix of financial and non-financial measures, namely:

1. return on net assets,
2. productivity,

3. safety,

4. quality,

5. on-time delivery and

6. scrap.

For example, in terms of reporting on safety performance, there was a weekly report comparing different plants in terms of accidents analysed by severity such as first aid, sent home and sent to hospital. Benchmarking within Case D was very important. The benchmarking proved to be particularly helpful when new plants were acquired because the benchmarking after the acquisition highlighted areas of difference requiring further investigation.

Another area of performance measurement was in relation to Case D's environmental performance. For example, Case D tried to identify opportunities to use less electricity and reduce gas emissions in its manufacturing operations. During the past year Case D has invested more than £1 million in more than 40 electrical efficiency projects. One interviewee mentioned that 'every worker is encouraged to be aware of energy consumption and to be innovative about ways to use energy more efficiently'.

Benchmarking within Case D was very important. The benchmarking proved to be particularly helpful when new plants were acquired because the benchmarking after the acquisition highlighted areas of difference requiring further investigation. This particular plant had one of the best levels of productivity within the group. Case D tried to 'do more with less' by concentrating on training to develop employees' knowledge and skills. This plant had the objective of achieving top quartile performance in benchmarking within the group. Case D had made progress in trying to link the effects of specific HR policies with its organisational performance by combining the results of its employee opinion surveys with its benchmarking results.

## 4.2.  Employees

All interviewees considered the role of employees in achieving Case D's budgeted performance to be extremely important, namely 7 on a scale of 1 (not important at all) to 7 (extremely important). Interviewees considered employees as 'assets' rather than 'costs'. As one interviewee said 'we would not be where we are today without our very committed and dedicated group of employees'. One problem for Case D is that within the next 10 years, more than 50% of employees will retire. The interviewees considered that a good pension scheme can help to improve organisational performance. Case D has also introduced a long-term plan to pass on knowledge and skills to younger employees using a 'buddy' training system.

## 4.3. Links between Management Accountants and HR Managers

Interviewees considered the most critical link between management accountants and HR managers to be the annual budget. This included discussions about setting the budget and then the reporting of actual results against the budget including analysis of reasons for the actual results being different from the budget. The number of employees and the required mix of skills were major points of discussion between HR managers and management accountants during the preparation of the annual budget.

In Case D the managers performed a number of HR functions usually undertaken by HR managers in other organisations so that the links between the management accountants and other managers covered some HR topics. The interviewees considered that the employees contributed most of Case D's value added.

## 4.4. HR Policies and Organisational Performance

In the 1990s, this plant had experienced severe problems and a new managing director was appointed to 'either turn the plant around or shut it down'. This had been a traumatic period for the plant's employees and all interviewees referred to it. The interviewees considered that this period in the 1990s had encouraged the development of much closer teamwork within the plant. The interviewees were in no doubt that effective teamwork was a major factor underlying the improved performance of this plant. Most of the interviewees also mentioned the improvements in Case D's pension scheme in recent years and how such changes had motivated employees to improve organisational performance.

Another factor behind the improved organisational performance of this plant was that there had been hardly any management turnover since the 1990s and there had been a concentration on 'making things better and learning new skills'. The interviewees considered that 'employee initiated training' and 'continual upgrading of skills' were important factors behind the continuing improvement in this plant's overall performance. One interesting feature of Case D was that there was no specific budget for training. Instead training was driven purely by employees' needs and demands.

Although Case D had experienced a reduction in the number of employees in the past, recently it had started a major recruitment drive, and interviewees considered that recruiting the best mix and quality of employees was critical for Case D's future performance. One interviewee stated that 'with the virtual doubling of employees and operations in the past year, new teams were introduced and built up' and other interviewees confirmed this point. Four-day training sessions were introduced to enhance employees' troubleshooting skills. The training sessions included both formal lectures and hands-on applications to solve common operational problems. The interviewees had no doubt that Case D's training was a major factor in improving its overall performance.

Case D operated on a decentralised basis with responsibility for performance resting mainly on the plant managers, and the underlying philosophy was that the plant managers should empower their employees to achieve the overall organisational target of a top quartile performance. All employees were involved in suggesting improvements and innovation opportunities. Without necessarily using the term 'employee empowerment', the interviewees emphasised that employee empowerment was another factor underlying the improved performance of Case D.

The interviewees all mentioned the good atmosphere or 'good culture' that now existed within Case D (usually mentioned in contrast to the 'bad culture' of the early 1900s). The good culture involved communication, low absenteeism, good union relations and excellent relations between the hourly paid and salaried employees. Several interviewees mentioned the importance of managers walking around the production floor every day. Again the interviewees considered that the 'good culture' of Case D was another factor influencing its improved performance.

## 4.5.  External Reporting

Most interviewees considered that HR and organisational performance information could be reported externally to shareholders and other stakeholders in Case D. Such externally reported information could be a mix of both qualitative and quantitative information. Qualitative information could include the four values (respect, progressiveness, integrity and open communication) that were already included in Case D's vision statement, results of its employee opinion survey and its training and other HR initiatives (such as teamwork and employee empowerment). Quantitative information could include employee demographics, safety performance and productivity statistics. Most interviewees suggested that it would be difficult, but not impossible, to link specific HR policies with improved organisational performance. Interviewees considered that statements could be made about top management's opinions on the impact of specific HR policies on organisational performance.

## 5.  Summary

The following findings emerged from Case D:

1. Employee opinion surveys can show the relationship between specific HR policies and organisational performance.
2. A performance and appraisal system supports the development of employees leading to improved organisational performance.

3. Performance is defined in terms of a combination of non-financial and financial measures.

4. The results of employee opinion surveys over a number of years can be combined with benchmarking results to explore the relationships between HR policies and organisational performance.

5. The role of employees is extremely important in achieving budgeted performance.

6. A good pension scheme can help to improve organisational performance.

7. When employees are viewed as assets (rather than costs), this has a positive impact on organisational performance.

8. The annual budget is an important channel of communication between HR managers and management accountants.

9. The recruitment of the best mix and quality of employees is critical for future organisational performance.

10. Effective teamwork is a major factor in improving organisational performance.

11. Employee initiated training leads to improved organisational performance.

12. Employee empowerment is a significant factor in improving organisational performance.

13. Good culture is an important factor underlying improved organisational performance.

14. Qualitative and quantitative statements could be made in the annual report about HR policies and their impact on organisational performance.

# Case E

## 1.  Research Site

Case E is a British software development company that has operated for about 20 years. There were less than 1,000 employees in the whole organisation and under 200 employees at the research site. The turnover for Case E was under £100 million. The total employee costs were approximately 70% of total costs.

At the research site there were two finance staff (including one management accountant) and two HR members of staff. Overall the interviewees considered the level of competition for employees for this research site to be very high (that is, 7 on a scale of 1 to 7).

## 2.  Interviewees

There were seven interviewees, namely non-executive chairman (with an accounting background), managing director, finance director, management accountant, HR director, HR manager and marketing director. All interviewees had a first degree or professional qualification and their experience in their current field of expertise ranged from 5 to 30 years with an average of more than 10 years. The interviewees had worked for Case E for between 2 and 20 years. Each interview lasted for about an hour and, in addition to the interviews and observation, the interviewees provided copies of a number of documents.

## 3.  HR Policies

Case E had developed a new niche in the software development market with yearly licences for their software and only one version of this specialised software with all clients receiving all the upgrades. Case E maintained the software and upgrades and provided a 'hot line service' for all clients to deal with any software problem. The clients determined the priority and timing of the upgrades to the software. Case E was very much a customer-driven company.

This business model had implications for the HR policies. Firstly, only a very small number of staff in the whole organisation had a complete overview of the software package. Obviously these staff members were key to the future of Case E and staff retention was critical. Secondly, the complexity of the software development meant that it took new members of staff 18 months of training before they became really productive. For a relatively small organisation, this meant that Case E had to forecast increased demand at least 18 months in advance to be able to recruit suitable employees in time.

Interviewees recognised the strategic need for a formal training programme but again the relatively small size of the organisation made it difficult to meet this need. Another strategic development recognised by the Board of Directors was the strengthening of the senior management team. Case E had begun to develop and promote lower level employees into senior positions and such promotions had an important motivational effect on other employees who saw the opportunity for future, internal promotion. The interviewees considered that the end result was improved organisational performance.

A great deal of emphasis was also placed on the training of sales employees in terms of their knowledge of the product (software program) including the detailed manual. In particular, sales employees had to be able to discuss with potential customers how this software program would affect and benefit that particular customer's business. The interviewees considered that this relatively recent emphasis on the training needs of sales employees had already had a significant positive effect on Case E's performance. Being a relatively small company, the interviewees said that they were able to see a clear link (with a short time lag) between effective training and improved organisational performance.

Given the size of Case E, the HR policies were less formalised than in the other five cases. This meant that Case E was able to react quickly to changing circumstances. However, Case E recognised that, as it grew, its HR policies would have to become more formalised and this was already happening in the training area.

## 4.   Findings

## 4.1.   Performance Measurement

Case E defined its performance by a mix of financial and non-financial measures. Interviewees considered that a mix of financial and non-financial performance measures helped to improve Case E's overall performance. The main financial measure was sales. Sales were analysed by:

- renewable licence fees for software and
- consultancy fees.

It was relatively easy to estimate the renewable licence fees but relatively difficult to forecast the future consultancy income. An important control ratio was the renewable licence fees in relation to Case E's fixed costs. Sales were budgeted by customer contract with monthly revisions. Being a relatively small company, cash flow was critical and monitoring actual cash flow against budgeted cash flow was significant. For each contract the customer paid 50% on placing the order, 25% on testing and 25% when fully online.

Non-financial performance measurements included customer satisfaction. Case E maintained a log of customer problems with their software and also asked each customer annually for their top five development needs in relation to the software. In addition, existing software quality was measured by the number of bugs found and the new development software was measured by failure at the customer's site either during the test phase or during final implementation. The performance of the sales personnel was measured by number of contacts, the success rate in turning such contacts into signed contracts and the time from the initial contact to the date of the signed contract. For a small company it was important to try to minimise the time between the initial contact and the date of signing the final contract (when the customer paid 50% of the contract value). With the timing of sales so important for the cash flow, Case E sets targets each month for completed sales. Commission for the sales personnel depended on both sales and the date of the customer signing the contract.

In addition to the above performance measures for the business as a whole, performance measures were also set by project and for each individual employee. For example, the number of projects managed by each project manager was monitored as was the progress of each project in order to meet the agreed delivery date of the software to the customer. Targets were set for employees in all functions including sales, software development, administration and support activities. There were 'employee of the month' and 'employee of the year' awards. However, as one employee said:

> the critical success factors for Case E are the price of each contract, the quality of the software and the delivery of the final version of the fully working software to the customer.

## 4.2.  Employees

Given the comparatively small size of Case E, it is perhaps not too surprising that all the interviewees talked about it being very much a family. The organisation itself was relatively young; many of the employees were comparatively young and had been with Case E since it started. The top managers tried to encourage this family atmosphere. The interviewees believed that this family culture increased employees' commitment and motivation and, as a result, helped to improve Case E's performance. As one interviewee said:

> the product itself (the software) requires everyone to do their job properly because if someone makes a mistake, this will almost certainly lead to a failure in the software program and this failure can be very expensive to correct either during the testing phase or the installation phase at the client's premises.

Another interviewee said that 'it is very much the case of doing everything right the first time'.

Although Case E had been in existence for about 20 years, some of its employees had been with it since its very early days. Case E had tried very hard, even during some difficult times, not to make employees redundant but recently this had proved impossible. However, employees obviously developed great loyalty to Case E and its expansion over the years enabled it to offer development opportunities to existing employees. Nevertheless, all the interviewees considered that this family culture had a very positive impact on Case E's overall performance.

## 4.3.    Links between Management Accountants and HR Managers

Given the size of Case E, there were very close links between the Finance Director and the HR Director. Indeed these two Directors had daily discussions. The budget was the most important link between these two Directors. With the 18 months training programme for new staff, it was critical that the budget took this fact into account. In other words, if Case E planned expansion, it needed to hire new employees almost 18 months in advance of such expansion. However, it was important for Case E not to hire too many new employees, so usually existing staff would be expected to take on some of the work for new contracts in addition to their existing duties. This enabled Case E to expand while at the same time reducing some of its risk. To date this expansion policy had been very successful for Case E.

The Finance Director had daily discussion with most other managers and also discussed the comparison of actual results against the budget with both the other directors and managers. The date when a customer signed a new contract was critical for Case E. As mentioned above, remuneration for sales employees depended partly on meeting target dates for contracts to be signed by customers. An efficiency measure was calculated based on the estimated time between the date of first contact with a potential customer and the date of that customer signing a contract and the actual time involved. Case E had a long-term relationship with relatively few customers, and the Marketing Director, HR Director and Finance Director worked together to ensure that the needs of these critical customers were met. A basic form of life cycle costing was used.

Another critical area for the Finance Director was cash flow forecasting and control because of the relatively small size of Case E. This involved the Finance Director working very closely with both the HR Director and Marketing Director. The number of employees and their remuneration was within the control of Case E but the cash inflow depended on the date that customers signed their contracts and the resulting payments to Case E on the basis of such contracts.

Although at times the relatively small size of Case E was a disadvantage, it had one big advantage, namely the ability to make quick decisions. In addition, the management control was relatively informal but the interviewees considered it to be effective. One interviewee stated that the employees were Case E's most important suppliers and all interviewees considered employees to be assets rather than costs. In addition, interviewees had no doubt that the employees created the greatest percentage of Case E's value added.

## 4.4.   HR Policies and Organisational Performance

The interviewees emphasised that the quality of Case E's software depended on the quality and efforts of its employees. Therefore, the HR policies were designed to hire high-quality employees and retain them. The interviewees considered the employees to have a dedicated team approach that improved Case E's overall performance. The company tried as far as possible to look after its employees and the employees appreciated this fact and, in turn, gave their full commitment to Case E. In addition, employees generally enjoyed their work and this overall approach made the tasks of the HR Director and the Finance Director much easier. The interviewees had no doubt that the selection and hiring policies and the employee retention policies had major positive impacts on Case E's overall performance.

Being a relatively small company, several interviewees suggested that it was easier to measure the impact of employees on organisational performance. On the monetary side, Case E had the usual annual salary review for all employees but also monthly awards and bonuses for exceptional performance by employees. The interviewees considered the monetary rewards to be important but most interviewees suggested that the non-monetary rewards (such as recognition and seeing the impact of their own efforts on Case E's overall performance) were at least as important as the monetary rewards in leading to improved organisational performance.

It was a policy of Case E to invite customers and potential customers to its head office to meet staff. This reflected the confidence of Case E in its own employees. The feedback from customers on Case E's staff was extremely positive and this was critical because the quality of Case E's software depended on the quality of work of its employees. The interviewees agreed that customers were impressed by the commitment of Case E's staff. For example, problems did not occur too often with Case E's software but when such problems did arise, Case E's employees took such problems very personally and would do anything that was needed to solve such problems.

Several interviewees made the point that the link between employees and organisational performance was clearly seen when the rare event occurred of an employee leaving Case E. When an employee left, the performance of Case E suffered in three ways. Firstly, Case E lost the knowledge and experience of an employee. Secondly, there was the cost and time spent in recruiting another high-quality graduate. Thirdly, there was the time and cost spent in training this new employee in Case E's software approach. The interviewees had no doubt that in Case E there was a direct link between HR policies (including recruitment and internal promotions) and its overall organisational performance.

## 4.5.  External Reporting

Most interviewees saw no major problems in Case E reporting externally qualitative statements about the impact of specific HR policies on its performance. However, the interviewees considered that it would be very difficult to report externally the monetary impact of specific HR policies on organisational performance. This was despite the fact that the same interviewees had no doubt about the link between specific HR policies and organisational performance. Most interviewees were clear that in the software industry generally, the success and failure of firms depended mainly on the quality of such firms' employees. The basic problem is providing sufficiently good 'hard evidence' that could be audited and reported externally.

## 5.  Summary

The following findings emerged from Case E:

1. The recruitment and retention of high-quality employees is critical to improve future organisational performance.
2. The development and promotion of employees has an important motivational effect that helps to improve future organisational performance.
3. There is a positive link (with a time lag) between effective training and improved organisational performance.
4. A mix of financial and non-financial measures helps to improve overall organisational performance.

5. A 'family culture' in an organisation can have a positive impact on organisational performance.

6. The budget is a significant communication link between management accountants and HR staff.

7. Teamwork is a factor helping to improve organisational performance.

8. When employees are viewed as assets (rather than costs), this has a positive impact on organisational performance.

9. Non-monetary rewards are as important as monetary rewards for employees in encouraging improved organisational performance.

10. There is a link between specific HR policies and improved organisational performance.

11. In an annual report, qualitative statements could be made about the impact of HR policies on organisational performance.

# Case F

## 1. Research Site

Case F is a listed British utility company that has operated for many years but was privatised in the fourth quarter of the twentieth century. There were approximately 2,000 employees at the case location which was the headquarters for this organisation with over 10,000 employees. The group annual turnover for Case F was over £5,000 million. The total employee costs were approximately 40% of controllable costs.

At the case location there were 40 finance staff (including 10 professionally qualified management accountants) and 10 HR staff out of the 2,000 staff. Overall the interviewees considered the level of competition to obtain staff for this research site to be very high (that is, 7 on a scale of 1 to 7).

## 2. Interviewees

There were seven interviewees being the group finance director, group HR director, two management accountants, an HR manager and two operational managers. All interviewees were graduates but the culture of this organisation was that they appointed those who could do the job regardless of their qualifications. For example, one of the HR interviewees had no formal HR qualifications but had previously been an operational manager with an engineering background. However, some other HR managers were HR specialists.

There was a culture of internal promotions with a few appointments from outside the group. All the interviewees had more than 15 years of working experience and had been employed by Case F for between 16 and 30 years. Such relatively long service with Case F was typical of the average employee. The average length of each interview was an hour and, in addition to the interviews and observation, copies of a number of documents were obtained.

## 3. HR Policies

Case F was interesting in that historically it had a large number of HR staff relative to other organisations of its size and relative to other utility companies. These HR staff had done a great deal of work to try to link changes in specific HR policies with overall organisational performances. Furthermore, Case F had entered into an HR benchmarking scheme with other organisations to give it another basis of comparison in relation to its HR policies and organisational performance. A few years ago Case F decided to adopt a different HR approach. The new approach aimed to cut the centralised HR costs by reducing the number of HR managers and redeploying existing HR staff – often into operational management roles. This new approach aimed to improve organisational performance, firstly, by reducing total HR costs and, secondly, by devolving much of the HR function (performed by HR specialists in other organisations) to individual operational managers. The interviewees stated that the overall HR service had improved while at the same time Case F's performance had also improved in terms of various measures such as stock market performance, profitability and employee satisfaction (as measured by employee surveys).

The overall philosophy was a centralised HR function covering employee relations, pay scale and bonus negotiations, pensions and payroll. The HR function at the operational sites (as distinct from the headquarters) had a very limited role concentrating on recruitment (against centrally agreed employee numbers) with one HR person to a thousand employees at operational sites. In summary, there was good HR knowledge and experience at the headquarters (dealing with pay, pensions and targets) and there was an HR specialist at each large operational site with the site director being in day-to-day control of the site HR manager.

A second major HR policy that most interviewees considered affected organisational performance was pensions. The HR interviewees at the head office estimated that they spent 25% of their time on pensions. Case F had two main pension schemes as follows:

1.  final salary (where the pension paid depended on the employee's salary during the final three years of their working life) and
2.  defined benefit started in the 1990s.

The interviewees in Case F considered that good employees were attracted by a good pension scheme.

The defined benefit pension scheme started with the employer and the new employee contributing an equal amount but after five years the employer's contribution became 150% of the employee's contribution and after ten years it became 200% of the employee's contribution. The interviewees considered that this defined benefit pension scheme encouraged employees to stay at Case F.

A third main HR policy (emphasised by interviewees in Case F as having a major impact on organisational performance) was recruitment of the correct number and mix of good quality employees. A fourth HR policy highlighted by interviewees was training and development. For many years Case F had spent much less per head on training than the industry average but recently it decided to increase its training expenditure per head to improve its level of customer service. Training budgets were set centrally at headquarters and managed by the HR managers at the various sites within Case F. Each October every business within the group made a submission in relation to the external training budget. The HR Department at the headquarters controlled the internal training budget. Training was the main HR policy explored in relation to organisational performance during this case study. In the past, Case F had established a very positive relationship between training and organisational performance using employee surveys and external benchmarking over a number of years. Case F monitored its recent increase in training expenditure against other organisational performance targets.

# 4.   Findings

## 4.1.   Performance Measurement

Case F followed what several interviewees termed a 'traditional or old fashioned' approach to performance measurement that the interviewees considered worked very well. The emphasis was on profitability with a top-down budget approach including targets set (without too much consultation) for managers. Case F used a number of performance measures including profitability and non-financial measures.

Each cost centre manager did provide a forecast that was an input into the budget process. The Board of Directors approved the final budget and after six months there was also a reforecast and the actual results were reported against this revised forecast. After nine months there was a further review of operational results that was used as a basis for the following year's budget. However, a form of zero-based budgeting was used to avoid simply adding a percentage to the current year's results for next year's budget. As one interviewee put it 'our performance reporting system is better that some sophisticated performance model (such as the balanced scorecard) that needs many HR professionals to operate it'.

Case F did use a number of non-financial performance measures such as the following:

- customer satisfaction (measured by surveys of customers),
- supply minutes lost per customer,
- number of supply interruptions per customer,
- number of formal complaints,
- number of customers gained and lost,

- number of employees,
- number of reportable and lost time injuries,
- days lost through sickness and absence,
- number of hours of overtime and
- number of reportable environmental incidents.

Efforts were made to link the above non-financial measures with the resulting financial performance of the organisation. For example, Case F monitored its increased training expenditure to ensure that, after a time lag, it led to increased customer satisfaction and to improved profitability.

The performance of individual managers was measured one-third on organisational performance (against specific organisational targets) and two-thirds on individual performance (against specific targets for each manager). The organisational scheme was based on a deferred bonus that depended on a weighted combination of the following:

1. total shareholder return (measured by its dividend and performance of its share price),
2. customer service (measured by an industry survey of customers) and
3. safety performance (measured by an industry survey of safety).

The specific individual targets for managers included both financial and non-financial performance measures. An example given of a non-financial target for a manager was to train a deputy to succeed to this position in three years' time. Generally the targets set for individual managers were linked to the organisation's overall performance targets, and the interviewees considered that the performance-related bonus scheme was an important factor underlying the organisation's continuing improvement in its overall performance.

## 4.2. Employees

All the interviewees mentioned the culture of the organisation and compared it to being in a family (in the sense of being supportive of each other). The family approach was extremely important for the top management team. Indeed, several interviewees suggested that this family culture was a major reason for Case F's good performance over many years.

Although there was a formal employee performance reporting system there was also a great deal of informal feedback on individual performance. The interviewees considered that this informal feedback on individual performance was as important as the formal feedback, and both types of feedback led to improved individual performance leading to improved organisational performance. All the interviewees stressed that for the evaluation of employees, overall performance was more important than their specific short-term financial performance. The value added of individual employees was not measured but their performance against specific targets was measured. Case F also used the utility industry figures that were publicly available against which it benchmarked itself.

All the interviewees agreed that employees were the most important critical success factor for the achievement of budgeted organisational performance. The interviewees had no doubt that top management regarded the employees as assets rather than just costs as demonstrated, for example, by the family culture. In Case F employee average service was more than 15 years. This was partly explained by the nature of the utility industry with its emphasis on technical expertise and knowledge of the industry. Furthermore, following privatisation the opportunities to stay with Case F increased because of its diversification policy into other areas of business. It was similar to a Japanese 'job for life' policy and fitted in with the 'family culture' of the organisation. Interviewees considered that this 'job for life' policy definitely had a positive effect on organisational performance (as evidenced by the analysis using employee surveys and external benchmarking over a number of years). Interviewees also considered that viewing employees as assets (rather than costs) had a positive impact on organisational performance in the long term.

## 4.3.    Links between Management Accountants and HR Managers

Within Case F there were very close links between management accountants and HR managers with the budget being a central communication, coordination and control tool. For example, the interviewees revealed that there was a very close working relationship between the group finance director and the group HR director on a day-to-day basis and between HR staff and management accountants at site level. HR staff and management accountants were involved in discussions about the long-term plan but particularly about the annual budget and the resulting actual performance including the achievement of strategic targets. The number and mix of employees were critical components of the annual budget. With the 'job for life' policy, existing employees were often trained to develop new skills required by Case F. However, many HR staff and management accountants had daily contact in a decision-making capacity such as the number of employees and the pay rates in different areas of the business. There was also discussion between HR staff and management accountants about performance measurement and, in particular, the interpretation of both financial and non-financial results for the bonus scheme.

## 4.4.   HR Policies and Organisational Performance

One example of this cooperation between management accountants and HR managers was the policy on training. For many years the organisation had spent much less per head on training than the industry average. Recently it decided to increase its training expenditure per head to improve its level of customer service but this increase was closely linked to other organisational performance targets. A major target was to improve customer service by reducing the employee turnover rate in Case F's call centres. Therefore, the following relationships were closely monitored: increased training costs leading to reduced employee turnover in call centres leading to increased customer satisfaction and reduced recruitment costs.

Case F measured customer satisfaction with a mixture of information including its own surveys of customers, industry survey of customers, customer feedback and formal customer complaints to the industry regulator. Of course, there was the usual problem of the time delay in such relationships but Case F was monitoring these relationships to ensure that the increased training expenditure led to positive results particularly in terms of greater customer satisfaction and reduced recruitment costs.

Another training example was that, in the past, Case F had problems with customer complaints with its outsourced sales force. As a result Case F was now training its own direct sales force and again was experiencing a reduction in the number of customer complaints. An operational manager provided another example of the links between training and improved organisational performance. This interviewee said that 'when I identify the problem, I consider investing in training'. He gave the example of the cost of faults that had been an ongoing problem. With the assistance of HR staff, he tackled the problem by introducing training for team managers in relation to team performance. This training had two effects, namely the team dealing with capital projects improved so that 'the team got it right first time more often' and the total number of faults decreased after this team training. Secondly, the team repairing the faults found that the training improved their performance so that the cost of repairing each fault decreased. The net effect was a dramatic decrease in the cost of faults after this training and this manager had evidence that this improved organisational performance could be traced directly to this investment in training.

The interviewees suggested that over a number of years the culture of Case F had become more open, honest and informal. Managers operated an open door system not only for those reporting directly to them but also for employees two or three levels below. The Chief Executive of the entire organisation also had a programme for going round all areas of the business and Case F also operated 20 Discussion Focus Groups. These groups included employees from all levels of the organisation and employees talked about whatever was concerning them about the organisation. Summaries of the discussion from these focus groups went to the top management. All the interviewees suggested that this family culture within Case F had led to improved financial performance of the organisation.

Another important HR policy linked to this family culture was that when jobs disappeared (for example by re-engineering) employees were not made redundant but went into a Resource Centre where other parts of the business would look first when vacancies for existing posts or new posts became available. Employees continued to be paid in this Resource Centre and were also offered further training or retraining. Existing employees were often retrained to develop the new skills required by Case F. In the monthly performance report for top management, there was a section on both the number and skills of employees in the Resource Centre and vacancies analysed, firstly, by business area and, secondly, by skill area such as engineer, craft, administration and management. In effect Case F had a form of 'job for life' policy that fitted in with its culture. As one of the Board of Directors said 'the family culture coupled with this job for life policy has a greater positive impact on our organisational performance than our very effective training and development'.

Case F considered itself to be successful and one measure of its success was that it had been in the top quartile for the utility industry for its FTSE performance over one, three and five years. The interviewees regarded Case F as a good place to work. Case F had a reputation for not overpaying but interviewees cited examples where employees of Case F had left to join another organisation but had returned to Case F.

Case F tried to make relatively quick decisions because of the rapidly changing nature of some areas of its business (such as energy prices) and accepted that some of its decisions would be wrong but overall it would benefit from its quick decision-making. There was a strong focus on controlling costs and a strong ethos of cross-functional team working. Several interviewees considered that this cross-functional team working had improved the financial performance of the organisation (as evidenced by the analysis using employee surveys and external benchmarking over a number of years).

## 4.5. External Reporting

Most interviewees considered that it would be difficult to report externally the quantitative impact of specific HR policies on organisational performance but some qualitative statements could be disclosed. For example, several interviewees suggested that statements could be reported externally about training and development and the effect on Case F's organisational performance. Similarly, some interviewees considered that statements could be made in the annual report about cross-functional team working and its effect on organisational performance. However, interviewees considered it much more difficult to report externally about the 'family culture' and its effect on organisational performance. As one interviewee put it:

> the family culture probably has more impact on our organisation's performance than our training and development but reporting on our family culture in our annual report would be like talking that you are in favour of motherhood.

## █ 5.  Summary

The following findings emerged from Case F:

1. Devolving some of the HR function to operational managers can lead to improvements in organisational performance.
2. A good pension scheme can have a positive impact on organisational performance.
3. A mix of financial and non-financial measures leads to improvements in organisational performance.
4. Benchmarking results can be combined with the results from employee surveys over a number of years to explore the relationships between HR policies and organisational performance.
5. Recruitment of good quality employees has a major positive impact on future organisational performance.
6. A 'job for life' policy has a positive effect on organisational performance.
7. When employees are viewed as assets rather than simply costs, this has a positive impact on organisational performance.
8. Budgeting is an important communication link between management accountants and HR managers.
9. Training has a positive impact (with a time lag) on organisational performance.
10. A performance-related bonus scheme can lead to improved organisational performance.
11. Organisational culture (such as a family culture) can have a positive impact on organisational performance.
12. Teamwork has a positive impact on organisational performance.
13. Qualitative statements can be made in an organisation's published report about the impact of specific HR policies on organisational performance.

# Cross-case Analysis and Telephone Interviews

## ▇ 1.  Cross-case Analysis

Table 1 gives a comparative summary of the organisational data from the six case studies.

After the six case studies were completed, a cross-case analysis was undertaken and the following 11 findings emerged to be tested during the telephone interviews in Canada, Japan and the UK:

1. A mix of financial and non-financial measures leads to improved performance.
2. The role of employees is critical in achieving an organisation's targeted performance.
3. Teamwork has a major impact on an organisation's performance.
4. Organisational culture (with regard to employees) has a major impact on an organisation's performance.
5. A pension scheme can have a major impact on an organisation's performance.
6. When employees are viewed as assets rather than simply costs, this has a positive impact on an organisation's performance.
7. There is a positive link between training and an organisation's performance.
8. A job for life policy:
     i.   encourages managers to take a long-term view,
     ii.  has a positive effect on an organisation's long-term performance,
     iii. increases the motivation of employees and
     iv.  increases loyalty from employees.
9. Benchmarking is a useful technique for exploring the relationship between HR policies and an organisation's performance.
10. Specific HR policies can be linked to an organisation's performance.
11. Statements could be made in an organisation's published report about the impact of HR policies on an organisation's performance.

The eighth finding above about a job for life policy was tested only during the Japanese telephone interviews.

**Table 1**   Details on Six Cases

|  | Case A | Case B | Case C | Case D | Case E | Case F |
|---|---|---|---|---|---|---|
| Country | Japan | Japan | Canada | Canada | UK | UK |
| Sector | Electronics | Consumer products | Building materials | Timber products | Software development | Utility |
| Years in existence | c100 | c100 | c100 | c100 | c20 | c100 |
| No. of employees in organisation | >100,000 | >25,000 | >10,000 | >5,000 | <1,000 | >10,000 |
| No. of employees at research sites | 1,500 | 2,000 | 1,000 | 300 | 200 | 2,000 |
| Turnover | >£10 billion | >£5 billion | >£5 billion | >£1 billion | <£100 million | >£5 billion |
| Employees costs as % of total costs | 30% | 30% | 35% | 30% | 70% | 40% |

# ▌ 2.   Findings from the Telephone Interviews

The 11 findings were turned into draft questions that were pilot tested with six prac-
titioners. After this pilot test, these draft questions were amended for the final telephone questionnaire. A random sample was taken from the top 1,000 companies in
Canada, Japan and the UK. The telephone interviewees in the companies selected
were finance directors or management accountants. If a company did not wish to
participate in the survey, the next company in the sample was selected until 40 telephone interviews were conducted in Japan, 30 in Canada and 30 in the UK (giving
a total of 100 interviews). The telephone interview results for the above case study
findings are summarised below under the following 11 sub-headings.

## 2.1.   Mix of Financial and Non-financial Performance Measures

Table 2 shows the performance measures used by more than 5% of the telephone
interviewees' companies in Canada, Japan and the UK. The companies in the telephone interviews used a variety of both financial and non-financial performance
measures in all three countries. Although almost all the companies used a mix

**Table 2**   Performance Measures Used

|  | Canada (30 interviewees) % | Japan (40) % | UK (30) % | Total number of interviewees (100) % |
|---|---|---|---|---|
| Profit | 50 | 65 | 50 | 56 |
| Return on capital | 43 | 25 | 40 | 35 |
| Customer satisfaction | 20 | 20 | 37 | 25 |
| Sales | 17 | 58 | 3 | 29 |
| Quality | 10 | 18 | 17 | 15 |
| Cash flow | 7 | 10 | 20 | 12 |
| Employee satisfaction | – | 15 | 3 | 7 |
| Employee turnover | 17 | – | 3 | 6 |
| Productivity | – | 15 | – | 6 |

**Table 3**   Mix of Financial and Non-financial Performance Measures

| Leads to improved organisational performance | 1 Strongly disagree | 2 Disagree | 3 Neutral | 4 Agree | 5 Strongly agree | Total |
|---|---|---|---|---|---|---|
| Canada | 0 | 0 | 7 | 7 | 16 | 30 |
| Japan | 1 | 1 | 8 | 21 | 9 | 40 |
| UK | 0 | 0 | 0 | 19 | 11 | 30 |
| Total | 1 | 1 | 15 | 47 | 36 | 100 |

of both financial and non-financial performance measures, Table 2 shows that at least half of the companies surveyed in all three countries used a profit performance measure. Return on capital employed was the second most popular performance measure in Canada (43% of the companies surveyed) and the UK (40%), but the second most popular performance measure in Japan was sales (58%). The other financial performance measure in Table 2 was cash flow (used by 20% of the companies surveyed in the UK, 10% in Japan and 7% in Canada).

Table 2 reveals that the most popular non-financial performance measure used in all three countries was customer satisfaction (37% of the companies surveyed in the UK, 20% in Canada and 20% in Japan). Table 2 also shows other non-financial performance measures being used, such as quality in all three countries, employee satisfaction in Japan and the UK, employee turnover in Canada and the UK and productivity in Japan. Further non-financial performance measures (used by less than 5% of the companies surveyed) included delivery, environment, market share, number of new customers and safety.

Eighty-three percent of the interviewees agreed that the use of a mix of financial and non-financial measures led to improved organisational performance (see Table 3). The differences between the responses in Canada, Japan and the UK were statistically significant at the 5% level, mainly because 100% (30) of the UK interviewees agreed that the use of a mix of financial and non-financial measures led to improved organisational performance against 77% (23) of the Canadian interviewees and 75% (30) of the Japanese interviewees (see Table 3 for full details).

## 2.2.   Role of Employees

Ninety-seven percent of the interviewees agreed that the role of employees was critical in achieving an organisation's targeted performance (see Table 4). The

**Table 4** Role of Employees

| Critical in achieving organisation's targeted performance | 1 Strongly disagree | 2 Disagree | 3 Neutral | 4 Agree | 5 Strongly agree | Total |
|---|---|---|---|---|---|---|
| Canada | 0 | 1 | 0 | 4 | 25 | 30 |
| Japan | 0 | 0 | 0 | 15 | 25 | 40 |
| UK | 1 | 0 | 1 | 7 | 21 | 30 |
| Total | 1 | 1 | 1 | 26 | 71 | 100 |

**Table 5** Teamwork

| Major impact on organisational performance | 1 Strongly disagree | 2 Disagree | 3 Neutral | 4 Agree | 5 Strongly agree | Total |
|---|---|---|---|---|---|---|
| Canada | 0 | 1 | 0 | 11 | 18 | 30 |
| Japan | 0 | 0 | 2 | 22 | 16 | 40 |
| UK | 0 | 1 | 3 | 9 | 17 | 30 |
| Total | 0 | 2 | 5 | 42 | 51 | 100 |

differences between the responses in the three countries were not statistically significant at the 5% level (see Table 4 for full details). Many interviewees emphasised the impact of recruitment decisions on future organisational performance.

## 2.3. Teamwork

Ninety-three percent of the interviewees agreed that teamwork had a major impact on their organisation's performance (see Table 5). The differences between the responses from the three countries were not statistically significant at the 5% level (see Table 5 for full details).

## 2.4. Organisational Culture

Seventy-five percent of the interviewees agreed that organisational culture (with regard to employees) had a major impact on their organisation's performance – with

**Table 6**   Organisational Culture

| Major impact on organisational performance | 1 Strongly disagree | 2 Disagree | 3 Neutral | 4 Agree | 5 Strongly agree | Total |
|---|---|---|---|---|---|---|
| Canada | 0 | 3 | 5 | 8 | 14 | 30 |
| Japan | 0 | 0 | 6 | 21 | 13 | 40 |
| UK | 0 | 2 | 9 | 14 | 5 | 30 |
| Total | 0 | 5 | 20 | 43 | 32 | 100 |

**Table 7**   Pension Scheme

| Major impact on organisational performance | 1 Strongly disagree | 2 Disagree | 3 Neutral | 4 Agree | 5 Strongly agree | Total |
|---|---|---|---|---|---|---|
| Canada | 0 | 0 | 3 | 14 | 13 | 30 |
| Japan | 0 | 9 | 18 | 11 | 2 | 40 |
| UK | 0 | 5 | 19 | 4 | 2 | 30 |
| Total | 0 | 14 | 40 | 29 | 17 | 100 |

a further 20% neutral (see Table 6). The differences in the responses between the three countries were statistically significant at the 5% level mainly because 85% (34) of the Japanese interviewees agreed that organisational culture had a major impact on their organisation's performance against 73% (22) of the Canadian and 63% (19) of the UK interviewees (see Table 6 for full details). The Japanese interviewees considered that organisational culture and, in particular, the way that employees were treated (for example, with a job for life policy) had a significant impact on their organisation's performance.

## 2.5.   Pension Scheme

Forty-six percent of the interviewees agreed that a pension scheme had a major impact on their organisation's performance – with a further 40% neutral (see Table 7). The differences in the responses between the three countries were statistically

**Table 8** View Employees as Assets or Costs

|        | Assets | Costs | Both | Total |
|--------|--------|-------|------|-------|
| Canada | 24     | 2     | 4    | 30    |
| Japan  | 28     | 11    | 1    | 40    |
| UK     | 25     | 3     | 2    | 30    |
| Total  | 77     | 16    | 7    | 100   |

**Table 9** Link between Training and Organisational Performance

|        | No | Yes | Total |
|--------|----|-----|-------|
| Canada | 0  | 30  | 30    |
| Japan  | 23 | 17  | 40    |
| UK     | 0  | 30  | 30    |
| Total  | 23 | 77  | 100   |

significant at the 1% level mainly because 90% (27) of the Canadian interviewees agreed that a pension scheme had a major impact on their organisation's performance against 33% (13) of the Japanese interviewees and 20% (6) of the UK interviewees (see Table 7 for full details). Obviously, there are costs associated with any pension scheme, and further research is required to investigate these differences in responses between the Canadian interviewees on the one hand and the British and Japanese interviewees on the other hand.

## 2.6.  Employees as Assets or Costs

Seventy-seven percent of the interviewees considered employees as assets, 16% as costs and 7% as both (see Table 8). The differences between the responses in the three countries were not statistically significant at the 5% level (see Table 8 for full details). Overall, those interviewees who considered employees as assets were in no doubt that this view helped to improve their organisation's performance in the long term.

## 2.7.  Link between Training and Organisational Performance

Seventy-seven percent of the interviewees considered that there was a link between training and organisational performance (see Table 9). The differences between the

**Table 10**   Effects of Job for Life Policy for 33 Japanese Interviewees

| Job for life policy | 1 Strongly disagree | 2 Disagree | 3 Neutral | 4 Agree | 5 Strongly agree | Total |
|---|---|---|---|---|---|---|
| (a) Encourages managers to take long-term view | 1 | 2 | 11 | 16 | 3 | 33 |
| (b) Has positive long-term effect on organisational performance | 0 | 1 | 16 | 15 | 1 | 33 |
| (c) Increases motivation of employees | 0 | 2 | 21 | 10 | 0 | 33 |
| (d) Increases employees' loyalty | 0 | 2 | 16 | 14 | 1 | 33 |

responses in Canada, Japan and the UK were statistically significant at the 1% level because all 30 British and 30 Canadian interviewees agreed that there was such a link but only 43% (17) of the Japanese interviewees agreed (see Table 9 for full details). It appeared that the Japanese interviewees placed more emphasis on organisational culture and their treatment of employees (such as a job for life policy) than on other issues such as training.

## 2.8.   Job for Life Policy

The following results on the job for life question are only for the 40 Japanese telephone interviewees. Eighty-three percent (33) of the Japanese interviewees claimed that their organisation had a job for life policy. Given the pressures on the job for life policy in Japan, it was perhaps surprising that 83% of the Japanese interviewees' organisations still had such a policy.

A sub-set of questions in relation to this job for life policy revealed the following results (see Table 10 for full details). Firstly, 58% (19 of the 33 Japanese interviewees whose organisations had a job for life policy) agreed that such a policy encouraged managers to take a long-term view (with 33% neutral). Secondly, only 48% (16 of the 33 interviewees) agreed that a job for life policy had a positive long-term effect on their organisation's performance (with 48% neutral). Thirdly, only 30%

**Table 11** Benchmark Performance Measures

| Benchmark Performance Measures | No | Yes | Total |
|---|---|---|---|
| (a) *Within the organisation* | | | |
| Canada | 19 | 11 | 30 |
| Japan | 20 | 20 | 40 |
| UK | 9 | 21 | 30 |
| Total | 48 | 52 | 100 |
| (b) *Against other organisations* | | | |
| Canada | 18 | 12 | 30 |
| Japan | 27 | 13 | 40 |
| UK | 3 | 27 | 30 |
| Total | 48 | 52 | 100 |

(10 of the 33 interviewees) agreed that a job for life policy increased the motivation of employees (with 64% neutral). Fourthly, only 45% (15 of the 33 interviewees) agreed that a job for life policy increased loyalty from employees (with 48% neutral).

## 2.9. Benchmarking

Fifty-two percent of the interviewees said that their organisation benchmarked its performance measures within the organisation (see Table 11). The differences between the responses from the three countries were statistically significant at the 5% level mainly because 70% (21) of the UK interviewees benchmarked internally against 50% (20) of the Japanese interviewees and 37% (11) of the Canadian interviewees (see Table 11 for full details).

Again, but with some different organisations involved, fifty-two percent of the interviewees replied that their organisation benchmarked its performance measures against other organisations (see Table 11). This time the differences between the responses from the three countries were statistically significant at the 1% level. There was a strong evidence of differences between the responses from the three countries mainly because 90% (27) of the UK interviewees benchmarked externally whereas only 40% (12) of the Canadian interviewees and 33% (13) of the Japanese interviewees did (see Table 11 for full details).

**Table 12**   Benchmarking, HR Policies and Organisational Performance

| Benchmarking is a useful technique for exploring the link between HR policies and organisational performance | 1 Strongly disagree | 2 Disagree | 3 Neutral | 4 Agree | 5 Strongly agree | Total |
|---|---|---|---|---|---|---|
| Canada | 0 | 2 | 8 | 9 | 11 | 30 |
| Japan | 0 | 7 | 18 | 15 | 0 | 40 |
| UK | 0 | 2 | 10 | 13 | 5 | 30 |
| Total | 0 | 11 | 36 | 37 | 16 | 100 |

Fifty-three percent of the interviewees agreed that benchmarking was a useful technique for exploring the relationship between HR policies and their organisation's performance – with a further 36% being neutral (see Table 12). The differences between the responses from the three countries were again statistically significant at the 1% level because 67% (20) of the Canadian interviewees and 60% (18) of the UK interviewees agreed that benchmarking was a useful technique for exploring the relationship between HR policies and their organisation's performance whereas only 38% (15) of the Japanese interviewees agreed with 45% (18) of the Japanese interviewees being neutral (see Table 12 for full details).

## 2.10.   Links between HR Policies and Organisational Performance

Sixty-two percent of the interviewees replied that their organisation tried to link specific HR policies with their organisation's performance (see Table 13). The differences in the responses between the three countries were statistically significant at the 1% level mainly because 88% (35) of the Japanese interviewees tried to link specific HR policies with organisational performance against 53% (16) of the Canadian interviewees and 37% (11) of the UK interviewees (see Table 13 for full details). This finding again highlighted the emphasis given by the Japanese interviewees to HR issues.

## 2.11.   Statements in Published Reports

Fifty percent of the interviewees agreed that statements could be made in their organisation's published report about the impact of their HR policies on their organisation's

**Table 13**   Link Specific HR Policies with Organisational Performance

|  | No | Yes | Total |
|---|---|---|---|
| Canada | 14 | 16 | 30 |
| Japan | 5 | 35 | 40 |
| UK | 19 | 11 | 30 |
| Total | 38 | 62 | 100 |

**Table 14**   Statements on HR Policies in Annual Report

| Could make statements in annual report about impact of HR policies on organisa-tional per-formance | 1 Strongly disagree | 2 Disagree | 3 Neutral | 4 Agree | 5 Strongly agree | Total |
|---|---|---|---|---|---|---|
| Canada | 0 | 0 | 11 | 6 | 13 | 30 |
| Japan | 1 | 4 | 15 | 17 | 3 | 40 |
| UK | 0 | 3 | 16 | 8 | 3 | 30 |
| Total | 1 | 7 | 42 | 31 | 19 | 100 |

performance – with a further 42% neutral (see Table 14). The differences in the responses between the three countries were statistically significant at the 5% level mainly because 63% (19) of the Canadian interviewees agreed that statements could be made in their organisation's published report about the impact of their HR policies on their organisation's performance against 50% (20) of the Japanese and 37% (11) of the UK interviewees (see Table 14 for full details).

# Conclusions

## 1. Limitations

This research project has several limitations. In any case study research, the results are specific to a particular site. There is also possible conscious or unconscious bias in the interviewers' interaction with interviewees. Case study results may be biased by the researchers' closeness to the situation and the researchers' bias in the collection and analysis of the data. In an attempt to minimise the effects of such limitations, two researchers conducted all six case studies and multiple sources of evidence were used during the six cases.

The telephone interviews also have limitations including possible non-response bias of the organisations that decided not to participate, the relatively small sample of interviewees in each country and again the possible bias in the interviewers' interaction with the interviewees. In both the case studies and the telephone interviews, it is important to remember that this report provides insights into what the interviewees believe about the relationship between HR policies and organisational performance.

## 2. Case Studies

All six case studies used a mix of financial and non-financial performance measures. In all six cases, important links between HR managers and management accountants were the annual budget and longer term strategic plans. In all cases, there were regular meetings where management accountants discussed with HR managers detailed analysis of the variances between actual and budgeted results. In Cases A, B, C and F, HR managers and management accountants worked closely together on the performance-related bonus scheme. An important communication link also existed between HR managers and management accountants in relation to decision-making.

The HR policies mentioned by the interviewees (in at least three of the six cases) as affecting organisational performance included:

a. recruitment

b. training

c. teamwork

d.  organisational culture (with regard to employees)

e.  job for life

f.  pensions

With the possible exception of the above job for life policy, different cultures did not appear to have a major impact on the efficacy of HR policies on organisational performance. Of course, interviewees in individual case studies mentioned other HR policies but the above six HR policies were highlighted in at least three of the six cases as having a direct effect on organisational performance.

## 2.1.   Recruitment

In all six case studies, interviewees considered recruitment decisions to be critical in relation to their organisation's future performance by hiring the necessary quality and mix of employees. In all six case studies, the employees were regarded as 'assets' who created additional value rather than 'costs' that the organisation had to recover. Although the interviewees suggested that, in the short term, viewing employees as assets led to increased expenditure such as increased training and other costs, in all six case studies, the interviewees considered that viewing employees as assets led to long-term improvement in their organisation's performance.

In Case B, one interviewee made the point:

*With our job for life policy, hiring a new employee is similar to a capital investment decision for a new machine of well over £1 million. In addition, if we do not like the machine we can always sell it but we have a new graduate for 40 years.*

In Case C, the plant was recognised within the group as having the best practices for hiring and developing employees. The view taken was that the managers understood best the knowledge and skills required for any post and, more importantly, whether a particular individual would fit into the culture of the team, and therefore, the managers were the best people to do the interviewing and make the hiring decision without any other HR input. All interviewees in Case C agreed that this hiring approach had been extremely successful as measured by the plant's operational and financial performance and its very low employee turnover during the past five years.

## 2.2.   Training

Interviewees in all six companies mentioned training. For example, the Canadian Case C had a big initiative on training. Existing employees were trained to develop new skills (including leadership and soft skills) and training firms ran workshops so that employees could become multi-skilled. The Canadian Case D had a very specific type of 'on-the-job training'. This involved identifying the knowledge required for specific jobs and giving a list of questions to employees to help them to identify for themselves where they had a specific knowledge gap. The employees themselves then took the necessary steps (including training courses) to bridge their knowledge gap.

In all six cases, the interviewees had no doubt that training had a positive effect (with a time lag) on organisational performance. A few years ago when Case A went through a difficult period, it increased its training budget to develop some new skills among its employees. To fund such training investment in the past, all employees in Case A agreed to take a small salary reduction. Several interviewees in Case A considered that its improving financial performance was linked directly to this specific increase in training a few years ago. One way that Case A was trying to assess the effect of its training on organisational performance was by surveying employees for their views. By comparing the results of such surveys over a number of years, Case A was attempting to link the effects of specific HR policies (such as training) with its performance trying to take account of any time lag.

In Case B, several interviewees considered that training increased the knowledge and skills of employees leading to increased customer satisfaction that in turn led to improved performance. In Case C, the training programme (particularly its supervisory training) at the research site had been identified as best practice within the entire worldwide group. Case C tried to link the output from its training to both organisational and individual performance in two ways. Firstly, it had a list of required skills for the future and monitored such skills emerging from its training programme against its organisational performance. Secondly, it required all employees to write a report both 30 days and 90 days after completing their training programme. These reports analysed how well that specific training programme met the employee's own personal development training contract that was linked to the performance of that particular individual.

In Case D, there was no specific budget for training and actual training was driven purely by employees' needs and demands. The interviewees had no doubt that 'employee initiated training' and 'continual upgrading of skills' were important factors behind the continuing improvement in Case D's overall performance. Case E was a relatively small company and interviewees saw a clear link (with a relatively short time lag) between training and an improvement in Case E's performance. Case F had decided recently to increase its training expenditure per head, but this increase was closely linked to other organisational performance targets. For example, a major target was to improve customer service by reducing the employee turnover rate in its call centres. Therefore, Case F monitored closely that, with a time lag involved, increased training costs led to reduced employee turnover in its call centres which in turn led to increased customer satisfaction and reduced recruitment costs.

## 2.3.    Teamwork

Interviewees in Cases B, D, E and F emphasised the importance of teamwork and its positive effect on organisational performance. In Case B, the interviewees suggested that teamwork came naturally to most Japanese employees. Case D had experienced financial problems in the 1990s leading to redundancies, but recently Case D had expanded with an emphasis on new teams being built up. Case E was a relatively small company and all the interviewees mentioned the importance of teamwork. In Case F, there was a strong ethos of cross-functional teams.

In Case B, the interviewees considered teamwork to be the HR policy with the second greatest positive impact on their organisation's performance after their job for life policy. In Case B, teamwork was encouraged at all levels of the organisation. In Case D, the early 1990s had been a traumatic period during the 'downsizing' and all the interviewees referred to that period. The interviewees suggested that this past experience had encouraged the development of much better teamwork. In Case E the interviewees pointed out that, given its relatively small size, it was easier to see the positive effects of good teamwork on its organisational performance. In Case F, the interviewees considered that the strong ethos of the cross-functional teams had undoubtedly improved the overall performance of Case F.

## 2.4.    Organisational Culture

In Cases C, D, E and F, the interviewees mentioned the development of organisational culture in relation to employees. In Case C, the group was trying explicitly to change its culture and the current programme was 'leader for tomorrow' involving more employee empowerment to develop a more performance-orientated culture. All the interviewees in Case D mentioned the 'good culture' that now existed within the organisation (usually mentioned in contrast to the 'bad culture' of the 1990s). This 'good culture' involved frequent communication, low absenteeism, good union relations and excellent employee relations. Case E was a relatively young organisation with relatively young employees and the top managers tried to encourage a family atmosphere. Although Case F was a relatively large organisation, the interviewees in Case F made very similar comments to the interviewees in Case E. All the interviewees in Case F mentioned the culture of the organisation and compared it to being in a family. The family approach was extremely important for the top management team of Case F.

The interviewees in Case C suggested that its 'leader for tomorrow' programme and its new performance appraisal system had helped to improve its overall organisational performance. In Case D, the change from the 'bad culture' of the 1990s to its existing 'good culture' was cited by interviewees as one of the major reasons for the improvement in Case D's performance in recent years. Case E had developed a family culture that had helped the organisation to improve its performance. A similar situation existed in Case F where all the interviewees mentioned its family culture (despite the relatively large size of this organisation) and emphasised its important contribution to organisational performance.

## 2.5. Job for Life

The two Japanese companies (Cases A and B) had a job for life policy, although this policy had come under increasing pressure in recent years from international competition and other factors. One British company (Case F, the utility) also had a form of job for life policy. Of course, employees did leave Case F but the average length of service was more than 15 years. When jobs did disappear in Case F (for example, after re-engineering), employees were not made redundant but went into a Resource Centre where other parts of the business would look first when vacancies arose for existing or new posts. Employees continued to be paid in this Resource Centre (sometimes for several months) and were also offered further training or retraining. With this policy, existing employees were often retrained to develop the new skills required by Case F. In the monthly performance report for top management, there was a section on both the employees in this Resource Centre and vacancies analysed, firstly, by business area and, secondly, by skill area such as administration, engineering and management.

In Case B, the interviewees considered that their job for life policy was the most important HR policy affecting organisational performance. Some readers may not be surprised by the job for life policy of the Japanese Cases A and B but may be surprised by such a policy in the British Case F. One obvious question is how successful is Case F with such a policy? The interviewees in Case F considered it to be successful and one measure of its success was that it had been in the top quartile for the utility industry for its FTSE performance over the past one, three and five years.

The interviewees in Cases A, B and F stated that their job for life policy led to additional costs in the short term but all the interviewees in Cases A, B and F had no doubt that the long-term benefits from their job for life policy outweighed the additional short-term costs. The interviewees considered that their job for life policy:

i. encouraged employees to take a long-term view;

ii. increased employee motivation;

iii. increased organisational loyalty from employees and

iv. had a positive effect on organisational long-term performance.

## 2.6.   Pensions

Interviewees in both Canadian cases (C and D) and in one British case (F) mentioned that a good pension scheme could have a positive impact on organisational performance. In Case C, most of the interviewees considered that its good pension scheme helped to motivate employees leading to improved organisational performance. In recent years, Case D had improved its pension scheme and most of the interviewees considered that Case D now had one of the best company pension schemes in Canada.

In Case F, the HR interviewees at the head office estimated that they spent 25% of their total time on pensions. The interviewees in Case F believed that good employees were attracted by a good pension scheme. Case F's defined benefit pension scheme started with the employer and the employee contributing an equal amount to the pension scheme, but after five years with the company the employer's contribution became 150% of the employee's contribution and after service of 10 years it became 200% of the employee's contribution. The interviewees in Case F considered that this pension scheme encouraged employees to be more motivated and to remain with the company. The interviewees in Case F had no doubt that its good pension scheme had a positive impact on its organisational performance.

## 3.   Practical Implications from Case Studies

Three main findings from these six case studies are of particular interest to HR managers and management accountants. Firstly, the four HR policies mentioned by most interviewees in the six case studies as affecting organisational performance were recruitment, training, teamwork and organisational culture (with regard to employees). Secondly, management accountants provided information for and worked very closely with HR managers to support the HRM function in improving organisational performance. Areas of collaboration were strategic planning, budgeting (including discussion of actual results against budget), development of performance-related bonus schemes and decision-making. Management accountants spent a great deal of their time providing information and helping HR managers with a range of decisions.

Thirdly, almost all the interviewees believed that HR policies affected organisational performance. The companies in this study had made great efforts to link specific HR policies with organisational performance – despite the problems of time lags and the number of other factors affecting organisational performance. For example, in the early 1990s, Case F entered into an HR benchmarking scheme with other organisations, and the management accountants and HR managers combined the results from this benchmarking scheme with the results from Case F's own annual surveys of employees' opinions. Case F analysed these combined results over several years so that it could establish relationships between specific HR policies and organisational performance. Case F had to do this analysis over several years in order to overcome the twin problems of time lags (for example, between the introduction of a new HR policy and its resulting effect on organisational performance) and the number of other factors affecting organisational performance. It is important to emphasise that Case F used a specific HR benchmarking scheme as distinct from a normal external benchmarking scheme used by some of the other cases in this study. This breakthrough for Case F in linking the effects of specific HR policies to organisational performance was achieved by very close cooperation between its HR managers and management accountants.

## 4. Telephone Interviews

After the six case studies were completed, a cross-case analysis was undertaken and 11 findings emerged to be tested during the telephone interviews in Canada, Japan and the UK. Each of the 11 findings was supported by at least three of the six case studies. One of the 11 findings about a job for life policy was tested only during the 40 Japanese interviews. The remaining 10 findings from the case studies were then tested in 100 telephone interviews in Canada (30), Japan (40) and the UK (30).

One finding from the case studies was not supported by at least 50% of the telephone interviewees, namely only 46% of the interviewees agreed that a pension scheme had a major positive impact on their organisation's performance (see Table 6 of Chapter 8). However, 90% (27) of the Canadian interviewees agreed with this statement against 33% (13) of the Japanese and 20% (6) of the UK interviewees. The rising cost of funding final salary pension schemes was mentioned by some interviewees.

Only the Japanese interviewees were asked about the job for life policy with 83% (33) of these interviewees claiming that their organisation had a job for life policy. Of these 33 Japanese interviewees whose organisations had a job for life policy, 58% agreed that such a policy encouraged managers to take a long-term view but only 46% agreed that such a policy had a positive long-term effect on their organisation's performance. Furthermore, only 30% of these 33 Japanese interviewees agreed that a job for life policy increased the motivation of employees and only 45% agreed that such a policy increased loyalty from employees.

The following nine findings from the case studies were supported by 50% or more of the telephone interviewees:

1. A mix of financial and non-financial measures leads to improved organisational performance.
2. The role of employees is critical in achieving an organisation's targeted performance.
3. Teamwork has a major impact on an organisation's performance.

4. Organisational culture (with regard to employees) has a major impact on an organisation's performance.

5. When employees are viewed as assets rather than simply costs, this has a positive impact on an organisation's performance.

6. There is a positive link between training and an organisation's performance.

7. Benchmarking is a useful technique for exploring the relationship between HR policies and an organisation's performance.

8. Specific HR policies can be linked to an organisation's performance.

9. Statements could be made in an organisation's published report about the impact of HR policies on an organisation's performance.

# 5.   Overall Findings

Firstly, the four HR policies mentioned by most interviewees in the case studies as directly affecting organisational performance (and confirmed by the results from the 100 telephone interviews) were:

1. recruitment,

2. training,

3. teamwork and

4. organisational culture (with regard to employees).

Almost all the interviewees considered that HR policies affected organisational performance.

Secondly, the evidence from the six case studies and 100 telephone interviews revealed that HR managers and management accountants were working very closely together with management accountants providing information for HR managers to support the HRM function to improve organisational performance. Examples of close cooperation between management accountants and HR managers included strategic plans, budgets, performance-related bonus schemes, providing information and assistance with decision-making and the example below of establishing links between HR policies and organisational performance.

Thirdly, the evidence from the six case studies and 100 telephone interviews revealed that HR managers and management accountants were beginning to make some real progress in this area of the links between HR policies and organisational performance. Perhaps the most important finding from this research project is that in some companies, management accountants and HR managers have been working very closely together over a number of years using benchmarking or employee surveys or a combination of both benchmarking and employee survey results to explore the links between HR policies and organisational performance. Of the six case studies, Case F had made the greatest progress in establishing such links between specific HR policies and organisational performance.

Overall, in the researchers' opinion, it is difficult to link the effects of different HR policies with organisational performance because of both the time lags involved and the number of other factors affecting organisational performance. However, it is only by working in this area that our knowledge will improve.

# References

Accounting for People Taskforce, 2003. Human Capital Management Reporting. HMSO, London.

Armstrong, P., 1995. Accountancy and human resource management. In: Storey, J. (Ed.), Human Resource Management: A Critical Text. Routledge, London.

Arthur, J.B., 1994. Effects of human resource systems on manufacturing performance and turnover. Acad. Manage. J. 37 (3), 670–687.

Bacon, N., Berry, R., 2005. Pursuing Shareholder Value: Implications for Human Resource Management. CIMA Research Executive Summaries Series, London.

Bartel, A.P., 1994. Productivity gains from the implementation of employee training programs. Ind. Relat. 33, 411–425.

Becker, B., Gerhart, B., 1996. The impact of human resource management on organisational performance: progress and prospects. Acad. Manage. J. 39, 779–801.

Berry, R., Bacon, N., 2002. Marshmallow land: Shareholder value management and human resource management. CIMA Research Update, September, 2–3.

Bratton, J., 1994. Human resource management in transition. In: Bratton, J., Gold, J. (Eds.), Human Resource Management – Theory and Practice. Macmillan, New York.

CFO Research Services and Mercer Human Resource Consulting, 2002. Human Capital Management: The CFO's Perspective. Mercer Human Resource Consulting.

Chartered Institute of Personnel and Development, 2003. Human Capital Taskforce, CIPD, London.

Delaney, J.T., Lewin, D., Ichniowski, C., 1989. Human Resource Policies and Practices in American Firms. US Government Printing Office, BLMR 173, Washington.

Dey, I., 1993. Qualitative Data Analysis: A User-friendly Guide for Social Scientists. Routledge, London.

Eisenhardt, K.M., 1989. Building theories from case study research. Acad. Manage. Rev. 14 (4), 532–550.

Ezzamel, M., Lilley, S., Wilkinson, A., Willmott, H., 1995. Practices and practicalities in human resource management. Int. J. Hum. Resour. Manage. 6 (1), 63–80.

Gerhart, B., Milkovich, G.T., 1992. Organisational differences in managerial compensation and firm performance. Acad. Manage. J. 33, 663–691.

Hendry, C., Pettigrew, A., 1986. The practice of strategic human resource management. Pers. Rev. 15 (5), 3–8.

Hendry, C., Pettigrew, A., 1990. HRM: An agenda for the 1990s. Int. J. Hum. Resour. Manage. 1 (1), 17–25.

Hiromoto, T., 1988. Another hidden edge – Japanese management accounting. Har. Bus. Rev. July/August, 23–26.

Huselid, M.A., 1995. The impact of human resource management practices on turnover, productivity and corporate financial performance. Acad. Manage. J. 38 (3), 635–672.

Ichniowski, C., Shaw, K., Prennushi, G., 1995. The effects of human resource management practices on productivity. NBER Working Paper 5333, Industrial Relations Centre, Queen's University.

Innes, J., Kouhy, R., Vedd, R., 2001. Management Accounting and Strategic Human Resource Management. CIMA, London.

Institute of Chartered Accountants in England and Wales, 2003. Briefing Document on Human Capital Reporting. ICAEW, London.

Kaya, N., December 2006. The impact of human resource management practices and corporate entrepreneurship on firm performance. Int. J. Hum. Resour. Manage. 17 (12), 2074–2090.

Lengnick-Hall, C.A., Lengnick-Hall, M.I., 1988. Strategic human resources management: A review of the literature and a proposed typology. Acad. Manage. Rev. 13 (3), 454–470.

Liao, Y., April 2006. Human resource management control system and firm performance: A contingency model of corporate control. Int. J. Hum. Resour. Manage. 17 (4), 716–733.

Nkomo, L., 1987. Human resource planning and organisational performance: An exploratory analysis. Strateg. Manage. J. 8, 387–392.

Pfeffer, J., 1998. The Human Equation. Harvard Business School Press, Boston.

Purcell, J., 1995. Corporate strategy and its link with human resource management strategy. In: Storey, J. (Ed.), Human Resource Management: A Critical Text. Routledge, London, 63–86.

Schuler, R.S., Jackson, W.E., 1987. Linking competitive strategies with human resource management practices. Acad. Manage. Exec. 1 (3), 207–219.

Schuler, R.S., Macmillan, I.C., 1984. Gaining competitive advantage through human resource practices. Hum. Resour. Manage. 23 (3), 241–255.

Spicer, B.H., 1992. The resurgence of cost and management accounting; a review of some recent developments in practice, theories and case research methods. Manage. Account. Res. 3 (1), 1–37.

Stiles, P., Kulvisaechana, S., 2003. Human Capital and Performance: A Literature Review. Accounting for People Taskforce, HMSO, London.

Ulrich, D., Geller, A., DeSouza, G., 1984. A strategy, structure, human resource database: OASIS. Hum. Resour. Manage. 23 (1), 77–90.

Wright, P.M., McMahan, G.E., 1992. Theoretical perspectives for strategic human resource management. J. Manage. 18 (2), 295–320.

Yin, R.K., 1994. Case Study Research Design and Methods. Sage, Thousand Oaks, California.

# Index

CPSIA information can be obtained at www.ICGtesting.com
Printed in the USA
LVOW12s1447071113

360324LV00013B/149/P